ESCAPE FROM ANARCHY
A Strategy for Urban Survival

⊢ESCAPE FROM ANARCHY:

A Strategy for Urban Survival

Alan Edward Bent

Foreword by George S. Blair

Memphis State University Press

Memphis

To the memory of my father

Table of Contents

Foreword

WITHOUT AGREEING on its logical causes or probable consequences, social scientists unite their voices to advance the theme that an urban crisis currently exists in the United States. The least pessimistic believe things are not quite as bad as they seem, but warn that the range of feasible measures for meeting serious urban problems is narrow and hardly any of the measures are acceptable. To the least optimistic, the urban crisis is the greatest domestic problem today and there is little hope that the "muddling through" mode of operating can last much longer.

Thus, social scientists appear to view the urban crisis as a prolonged period of city illness which might mean slow, lingering paralysis or certain, creeping death. The alternatives are hardly those associated with a crisis in its medical context. For doctors, a crisis represents that change in a patient's progress which indicates that the result is to be recovery or death. In its non-medical use, crisis typically refers to a decision juncture or a turning point. But in its urban setting, crisis appears to offer no real choice for a positive prognosis to many social scientists. Nor does their use of the word connote that a turning point is at hand but rather that deterioration will continue.

While Alan Bent avoids the use of the word crisis in his study to a rewarding degree, his anxiety about and concern for the crisis identified by others come through clearly. But the alarm and despair in many urban analyses is replaced by a ray of hope and a design for survival in Bent's appraisal.

Since he utilizes many of the sources drawn on by others and relies on the same statistics, in part, how does Bent arrive at a strategy for urban survival while others doubt that the urban community can, or even should, survive? One of the effective weapons in his analytic arsenal is his careful use of more sophisticated research schemes. Applying the theoretical framework of systems models and cybernetics analysis, Bent develops an intersystem linkage between the urban and political systems by focusing on the performance, promise and potential of planning as the variable to provide this intersystem linkage.

The result of this analysis is a refreshing discovery that the ingredients of the metropolis that lead to the crisis also contain the potential for overcoming that crisis. The problems of people, limited resources, fragmented government, leadership void, and uncertain guidance by higher levels of government are very real. But they aren't hopeless. Rays of hope can create a beam of promise and potential. Bent sees the rays of hope and combines them into a strategy for restoring our metropolitan areas to fulfill the promises that appeared to be there and served as magnets to attract the millions who have been added to our large urban areas in the years following World War II.

Bent's strategy is one of forcing local government to be strong—even against its will, if necessary, so it can be a meaningful partner in our federal system. His five-level schema is an unrecognized reality because there is a regional government of sorts between the states and the national government and also between a state and its individual units of local government. Known variously as compacts, authorities, commissions, agreements, districts, councils, associations, etc., the rudiments of these two regional layers exist and are functioning. Bent's plan is to recognize them and enable them to function more adequately.

The particular strategy for urban survival proposed by Bent is a perceptive, carefully considered one. Essentially, it believes that rational inputs into a rational decision-making system should result in rational policies as outputs. What he advances as rational inputs will be viewed less admirably by some. The rationality he ascribes to our current system of decision-making will not be shared by all. Nor will his rational policy outputs be recognized as such universally. But his strategy should be considered in terms of its intended goal and the likely consequences that would follow its achievement or accrue if achievement fails.

Escape from anarchy will be viewed as a negative goal by those who profit from the confusion that current fragmentation produces, who realize the enactment of policies they favor, and who benefit from the absence of those that would be inhibiting. But too many local governments can result in too little local government for the general good of the citizenry. Bent sees this as a problem and proposes his best thinking to meet it in a way that restores vigor to both local and state governments. What he proposes is an intergovernmental hierarchy that recognizes the interrelatedness of people, economic activities, social institutions, and communications flow. The recognition of the interrelatedness results in the enactment of intergovernmental policies and the initiation of intergovernmental actions to meet the challenges of urban chaos, the destruction of the physical environment, and the atrophy of the values and mores of civilization.

Instead of assuming the posture of a benevolent bulldozer determined to destroy local government through governmental centralization and intervention, Bent recognizes that people make both slums and civilization. His strategy aims to advance the cause of civilization. The governmental intervention he proposes is as a countervailing force to serve public purposes. The degree of centralization is that which he sees essential if governmental inertia, for whatever reason, is to be replaced by positive governmental actions. Hopefully, readers will focus on the aim of the strategy as well as its methods, and his distractors will strive to improve upon his methods since his goal is worthy of the best efforts of all.

—George S. Blair

Introduction: A Calculus of Change

FUNCTIONS AND structures of government do not often anticipate changes in the environment; they manage to adjust to persistent exigencies with a patchwork of responding institutions. This is especially true of democracies characterized by pluralistic politics. The process of "muddling through" was reasonably satisfactory in earlier times when change was slower, institutions less monolithic and controlling, and the role of government less demanding. But today an unprecedented acceleration of change affecting every aspect of human experience and existence challenges the viability of a slowly responding political system.

The American polity was born in optimism in a day of limitless frontier and faith in boundless energy and individual self-determination. The creators of the polity—the Founding Fathers—sought a government that would least interfere in the "inevitable" course toward the good life, and guarantee the liberty of men now free to pursue their happiness. But soon after the realization of the polity, forces of historic change made the American dream a tired illusion.

The rural nation became an urban one. Open space and an aggressive spirit of undaunted optimism turned into jungles of concrete and steel, of pollution and waste, and fortresses of fear bespeaking the return to nature of the inhabitants. Industrialism, population growth, and organizational factors led to undesigned concentrations of men and machines. The urban mass grew unplanned and unguided, feeding on itself, and continues to grow to perhaps unimaginable proportions.

The complexities of the new urban republic and the velocity of contemporary change impose upon government a need for unparalleled energy. This posits a requirement for institutional flexibility and adaptability to maintain parity with environmental changes and provide the needed guidance for rational development. Under these new conditions of dynamic change government must undergo a continuous process of adaptiveness, responsiveness, exploration, and learning. And this is to be accomplished in the real-world environment of competing interests and clients in a pluralistic democracy.

> "In a situation of accelerated change and only limited autonomy, this will require a tightening of the feedback loops of information about change in both internal and environmental states, a general attitude of openness towards the future, and a quickening of the response times to new learning. All this hints at the need for far-reaching changes in the structure and processes of organizations that, for the most part, continue to behave as fairly bureaucratic, inflexible automatons programmed to only a thin repertoire of action responses."[1]

This is an analysis of the adaptiveness of American governmental institutions to urban processes of change. Adaptiveness to change necessitating political growth or adjustment is a condition of systemic modernization. The American po-

---

[1] John Friedmann, "The Future of Comprehensive Urban Planning: A Critique," *Public Administration Review*, No. 3, May/ June 1971, p. 321.

litical system bears scrutiny for its capability to respond to a new scope of problems—for its ability to modernize.

The sudden transformation of the living environment with its attendant perplexities questions the resourcefulness of existing institutions. In view of this, the pronouncement that "these states of Western Europe, North America, and the English-speaking dominions of the British Commonwealth 'need not aspire to modernity. They are modern. It has become part of their nature to be modern and indeed what they are is definitive of modernity.' "[2] cannot go unchallenged. Modernization is not a static state which, once realized, need never be initiated again. Environmental processes are dynamic and this necessitates continuous systemic changes for adaptiveness. It is not enough to assert that a system's persistence is proof of its modernity. Inefficient systems, by maintaining a political identity through time, manage to persist. Modernity can only be upheld when a political system has acquired the capability to respond effectively to changes in the environment.

Political modernization in response to new exigencies may, in addition to political alterations, require complementary social, economic, and demographic changes. The course of these innovations, if pursued rationally, posits a strategy for development. Political development is the process by which goals and institutions requisite for modernization are ordered. Rationality in modernization necessitates institutions appropriate for maximizing development goals. Conventionally, attention is focused on administrative institutions as rational imperatives for the attainment of goals in the modernization of the political system.

The administrative processes potentially conducive to the realization of development objectives can be better understood within the context of the total political system. The conditions found within the larger political system influence the ad-

[2] Ferrel Heady, *Public Administration: A Comparative Perspective,* Foundations of Public Administration Series, (Englewood Cliffs, N.J.: Prentice-Hall, Inc., 1966), p. 33, citing Edward Shils, *Political Development in the New States* (The Hague: Mouton & Co., 1962), p. 10.

ministrative procedures and arrangements in fulfillment of development goals. An effort is made to provide a holistic view of conditions in the urban system compelling the need for political modernization as well as a holistic view of the political system with its breadth of involved actors and institutions. The ecological approach of the analysis, relating a systemic process of modernization to environmental conditions and influences, requires a macroanalytic perspective. However, macroanalysis is furnished only as a result of examining relevant governmental subsystems and their interactions, insofar as their applicability to conditioning the urban system. Furthermore, analysis is not confined to political actors and processes alone but includes the differentiated, micro- and macro-decisions of private groups and institutions. This is especially crucial since the development of the existing urban pattern can be partially attributed to individualistic self-seeking.

The analysis and prescription are contained within a heuristic intersystem-analysis framework. This is done in order to develop a model by which to measure modernization. Other than this convenience, the analysis relies upon first-hand observations and other empirical evidence related to the systems examined. Empirical evidence and normative judgments influence the assessment of governmental adaptiveness—political modernization—leading to a prescriptive conclusion.

The utilization of an intersystem-analysis paradigm and several salutary references to systems analysis, computer science, and the latest advances of management science, are not to be construed as endorsements of mechanistic techniques as panaceas for urban problem solving. To the contrary, although there are no readily available panaceas there must be readily educated humanists. Systems analysis and management and computer science should be utilized as useful techniques in behalf of civilization. But, it is in the harmony of humanism and science that the urban republic may achieve its *eudaemonia*.

There is an excessive reliance in our society upon machines and technology, and the men and institutions that breed them.

Technology in pursuit of mechanistic efficiency has often been the catalyst for the explosion of change and growth. Too often, however, this has been accomplished at the expense of human values and needs. The relation of man to technology and science must clearly allow man the position of master. Growth and development should be guided by human considerations and in the event that continued growth prove detrimental to human needs then it should be arrested or excised.

Centralizing tendencies of modern society have created behemoth institutions—both private and public—with controlling influence over the aggregate values and mores of society. Amorphous bureaucracies striving for optimization through machine-like precision are characterized by their dehumanizing proclivities and their parochial interests. This aggravates human considerations when these are in conflict with institutional goals upheld by conventional symbols. Additionally, powerful interests and institutions have resources and political currency at their disposal, afforded by the economic system and the "exploitable fissures" of the American political system. In the face of these realities, there appears scant recourse to continued unchecked aggrandizement.

This is not intended as a revolt against the bureaucratic essentials set forth by Max Weber in the previous century, nor as a challenge to bureaucracies, as such, since they are indispensable in mass society. This is a call for a balanced orientation in men and institutions. The tremendous growth of organizations has led to an almost universal subordination of the self to the institution. This is the century of the triumph of institutions over men: never have so many been so dependent upon so few. Government provides but a few of the institutions that dominate our bodies and our secular souls. In fact, an arguable proposition would be that the institutions of government have been the least effective in guidance and control because of their power diffusion and inertia. In this age of massive organizations it necessitates the injection of the public sector as a countervailing force against private institutional arbitrariness while requiring political and self-controlling mechanisms to insure public institutions' responsibility and accountability.

An example of governmental beneficence in behalf of the individual is the passage of laws governing employment in the private sector which guarantee minimum wages, some semblance of human dignity, and proper working conditions. This study tries to tempt the need for government as a more effective countervailing force against the myriad enemies of the urban republic. Our government will be as effective as we, the people, will allow it to be. Humane and rational applications to the development of our total living environment are as necessary as humane rules in our work environment. Clearly, the task of government is to govern.

Intersystem-analysis

The analysis of the adaptiveness of American governmental institutions to urban processes of change is focused on the functions, constraints, and potential of public management of the urban system. The study applies the theoretical framework of systems models and cybernetics analysis in building an intersystem linkage between the urban system and the political system, operant within the matrix of our national social environment.[3] The intersystem model provides the basis for assessing systemic modernization. Planning, as a function of government management, is chosen as the variable conducive to providing the intersystem linkage.

"An intersystem framework involves two open systems connected to each other. Linkages or connections represent the lines of relationships of the two systems. The intersystem framework is not significantly different from the system-subsystem framework, but tends to focus on the

[3] Although the analysis of urban phenomena is applicable to other comparable societies, this study is limited to the American republic because some of the unique features of our political system are not transferable to the other systems Furthermore, the boundaries of the environment analyzed are expressly defined in order to enable the manageability of variables.

interdependence of systems and on the conjunctive (supporting) and disjunctive (conflicting) linkages."[4]

The urban system is characterized as dynamic and unstable. The political system is then examined for its adaptiveness to the changing conditions in the urban system. Adaptiveness is a process of the administrative imperatives of goal-seeking and goal-setting through communication and control. This intends the achievement of a cybernetic feedback loop of information about environmental and internal change in order to effect an integrated pattern of system-subsystem outputs to a desired terminal point. The controlled cybernetic process is the means by which the political system is able to adjust its structures and its goals in response to information regarding goals approximation.

Adaptiveness enables a system to persist through time in a dynamic environment. Persistence is achieved by a system's ability to alter its structures and functions in accordance with environmental conditions. The conduct of a social system's adaptiveness is analogous to a process of morphogenesis—the course of discovering new equilibria in an unstable environment. A political system's persistence within a morphogenic context of adaptiveness posits the creation, elaboration, or alteration of the system's structures, under appropriate feedback control.

A system's overall performance is analyzed through consideration of its essential "parts;" its goals, constraints, resources, components, and management. The key element of the system's parts is systems management. Management engenders plans setting the component goals, allocating resources, and controlling the system's execution. The system's goals are strategic objectives on whose behalf the system's components and resources are activated; the performance of the system is a measure of the advancement of subsystems toward selected

[4] Kenneth L. Kraemer, "The Planning Subsystem #9," *A Municipal Information and Decision System*, Vol. II, *Vertical Subsystems* (Los Angeles: Municipal Systems Research, University of Southern California, School of Public Administration, 1968), pp. 4–5.

goals. The resources are the system's general reservoir providing for component activity. Components are the functional subsystems within the total system that contribute to overall system rendition.[5]

This analysis is concerned with the linkage of the urban and political systems and identifies the systems management process as capable of effecting intersystem integration. Systems management is the rational course for a system's adaptiveness to environmental conditions; and requisite to rational management is a perspicacity in establishing and implementing goal-plans.

The triggering device of the adaptive process is planning. Planning is identified as the requisite administrative function keyed to effective adaptiveness because of latent and manifest contributions to strategies for change. In its preparation of proposals for action and strategies for change, planning provides the initial output of the political system, impelling the chain of ensuing goal-seeking activities. Hence, planning is the function that is intrinsic to rational systems management and has the capacity to perform a conjunctive role in the interaction of the systems insofar as it is joined to the action foci of the political system.

Calculus of Change

In this study systems are perceived as open-ended with interchanges between the systems and with the environment. This interchange generates a constant flow of activities and influences inherent in systems viability, self-transformation, and persistence.[6] A closed system's response to environmental stress or intrusion is either to increase in entropy to the eventual dissolution of the system or to adapt by restoration of a pre-existing point of equilibrium. An open system, however, adapts

[5] C. West Churchman, *The Systems Approach* (New York: A Delta Book, Dell Publishing Co., Inc., 1968) .

[6] Walter Buckley, *Sociology and Modern Systems Theory* (Englewood Cliffs, N.J.: Prentice-Hall, Inc., 1967); David Easton, *A Systems Analysis of Political Life* (New York: John Wiley and Sons, Inc., 1967).

to its environment by elaborating or altering its structures to a new level of complexity.

Karl Deutsch suggests that intrinsic to cybernetics is a systemic communications network, keyed to a feedback loop, that serves the persistence of a system by ordering appropriate changes in the system's structures.[7] Cybernetics, in this sense, provides the mechanisms of systemic "control," the self-steering of a system in adaptation to the dynamics of its environment. It is the process of adaptive evolution by the continuous creation and elaboration of structures. A cybernetic communications system affords processes of growth for the system. Growth, in addition to the attainment of maximum levels of systemic unity and self-determination, should also be reflected by changes in performance characteristics, and increased system openness through intensified channels of information intake about the environment. There should be an augmented capacity for goal attainment, through an increased ability to respond to environmental needs and to induce concomitant changes in the environment. Finally, growth should entail the ability for a system's re-ordering and expansion of goals.

The self-steering characteristic for cybernetics is guided by a feedback loop of decisive actions. The efficacy of system autonomy—or self-steering—through feedback, is dependent upon the system's receiving of three kinds of inputs: information of the external world; information of the past, with a generous capacity for its recall and recombination; and information about itself and its own parts.[8] Armed with this information, the goal-seeking, steering system will be charged by its own demands to respond to perceived changes in system or environmental circumstances. The goal-seeking system will designate its "target" and execute its output, which triggers the feedback sequence. The next stage of the sequence of goal-seeking performance will be determined by the acqui-

---

[7] Karl W. Deutsch, *The Nerves of Government, Models of Political Communication and Control* (New York: The Free Press, 1966); Gerald Jordan, "Three Models of Political And Social Thought," *Administrative Law Review,* Vol. 22 (June, 1970).

[8] Deutsch, p. 129.

sition of information about the goal and its own behavior and placement relative to it.

> In this manner, it will receive information concerning its own distance from the goal, or the extent to which it has already overshot the mark; and under certain conditions this information may serve to correct its approach and to guide it through a series of diminishing mistakes until the goal is reached. An extended organization of this kind may be able to alternate between the pursuit of a series of goals, or to rearrange under certain conditions parts of its own inner structure in such a manner that it may come to seek new goals.[9]

A political system, if characterized as constructively adaptive and goal-oriented, will strive to direct its energies and resources to act upon and modify conditions it encounters. The activity is distinguished as the outputs of the system.

> [Taking] the system rather than the environment as the starting point, outputs serve to conceptualize the ways in which the system acts back upon the environment and indirectly, therefore, upon itself . . .[10]

The process of adaptation is basic to systems persistence through time, in the face of environmental stress. For the political system, persistence is linked to its capacity as an open, self-regulating, and goal-setting system, to change itself. The measure of a political system's viability is seen through its adaptiveness which can be tested by identifying and following through the consequences of the outputs of its various parts.[11]

The political system's outputs and their outcomes provide the stimuli for the affected environment's feedback response. It is the feedback process that is crucial to systemic adaptiveness.

> Feedback can thus be seen as a central condition for all self-transforming . . . systems. Without the availability of returning information about experience with goals,

[9] *Ibid.*, pp. 219–220.
[10] Easton, *op. cit.*, p. 345.
[11] *Ibid.*, pp. 345–346.

transformations of goals themselves would only be random and possibly quite disjunctive with current or past experiences. With feedback, such experiences can be related to the continuous revisions for future long-run hopes, anticipations, and possibilities.[12]

Information is the regulator of the feedback loop. A political system's effectiveness in dealing with environmental conditions is related to the quality and quantity of information that it has on the existing state of the system and its environment, and about actual and anticipated outputs and their consequences.

If feedback—both information and responses—did not exist, the system would find itself utterly exposed to the vagaries of chance.

With feedback . . . the system is able to acquire some idea of how close it has come to its objectives and, if it desires to achieve a better approximation and has the capabilities for doing so, it is in a position to seek to modify its behavior with this end in view. Without feedback, each output would be completely independent of the other; with feedback, outputs may be highly interrelated, cumulative, and consistent . . . Returning information about the state of the system, its distance from desired goals, and about past and continuing effects of action already taken, enables the decision centers of the system to engage in any corrective action perceived as feasible and necessary to achieve the goals.[13]

True feedback cycles, in the cybernetic sense, require "internal mechanisms which measure or compare the feedback input against a goal and pass the mismatch information on to a control center which activates appropriate system counter behavior."[14] The internal control function of a system is a system management observance which, according to the late Norbert Wiener, is analogous to the steering of a ship:[15]

---

[12] *Ibid* , p. 371.
[13] *Ibid.,* pp. 367–703.
[14] Buckley, *op. cit.,* p. 69.
[15] Churchman, *op. cit.*

The captain of the ship as the manager generates the plans for the ship's operations and makes sure of the implementation of his plans. He institutes various kinds of information systems throughout the ship that inform him where a deviation from plan has occurred, and his task is to determine why the deviation has occurred, to evaluate the performance of the ship, and then finally, if necessary, to change his plan if the information indicates the advisability of doing so. This may be called the "cybernetic loop" of the management function, because it is what the steersman of a ship is supposed to accomplish.[16]

Planning is central to systems management in that it is indispensable to coordinated and guided policy outputs. Planning gives meaning to the cybernetic loop because it provides the system with goals against which to measure its performance, and for which it mobilizes its components and resources. Finally, the managed feedback loop provides the system persistence intelligence on goal-direction so that the system may morphogenically adapt to the environment. It is goal-oriented outputs that activate an adaptive system; and planning is the essence of rational and cohesive goal-seeking.

It is imperative to proclaim that the goals of a system contain normative aspects which most of the members of the system would like to pursue. Normative aspects are the basic values, norms and attitudes of a social system and condition such value considerations as "the good life" and morality. A system's adaptive process is not just a mechanical response to a mechanical feedback of the environment but also, critically, is response to normative conditions. It is, therefore, crucial for managers and other actors in the political system to constantly keep in mind the needs, expectations, and preferences of every member of the system as human individuals. A system's goals and goal-seeking, albeit facilitated by mechanistic attributes, must be adjusted to the normative needs of the social environment.

An inquiry into the outputs generated by the components of the political system, and its institutional structures' elabora-

16 *Ibid.,* p. 46.

tion, transformation, and creation, offers a gauge of the system's dynamic goal-seeking behavior. Assessment of intersystem linkage will be provided by an examination of the planning process's influence in goal-defining and goal-seeking, and of system management's communication and control procedures for the realization of a cybernetic feedback loop. The evaluation of whether, in the political system, there now exists a cybernetic loop for purposive goal-seeking will be derived by the measure of empirical conditions against the following paradigm of a cybernetic system:

1) A control center establishes certain desired goal parameters and the means by which they may be attained; 2) these goal decisions are transformed by administrative bodies into action outputs, which result in certain effects on the state of the system and its environment; 3) information about these effects are recorded and fed back to the control center; 4) the latter tests this new state of the system against the desired goal parameters to measure the error or deviation of the initial output response; 5) if the error leaves the system outside the limits set by the goal parameters, corrective output action is taken by the control center.[17]

[17] Buckley, *op. cit.,* p 174.

I

Ecology of Change

The State of the Systems

URBAN ENVIRONMENT has traditionally been defined in the purely physical terms of buildings, equipment and high density population clusters. The environment under these circumstances assumes discrete areal delimitations as well as a taxonomy based on gradated densities. The gauge of urbanism follows a pattern of concentric physical compactness, within an environment, peaking at a nucleus of residence, industry, and trade. This static, locational, and physical consideration of urbanism understands the pattern in terms of statistical units of settlement reflecting distinct distributions of population and energy. Considerations of interactions are typically microanalytic and confined to spatial proximities. Settlements receive neat classifications of urban intensity according to degree of physical and population convergence, ideally represented by a center of highest intensity surrounded by communities of gradually declining urbanness. Thus, the urban place, of communities formed into towns, cities, and in the aggregate, the metropolitan region, is a physically distinct entity and discernible as such from the air.

The static, locational, and physical emphasis of the urban envionment, however, omits the quintessence of urbanism. Cities, and their extent, became the hubs of civilization as diverse groups and institutions mixed in physical proximity to form a unique quality and diversity of life. Physical propinquity had become essential to facilitate frequent contact among specialized, and thereby interdependent, households and businesses. Thus, the maturation of the urban environment, in essence, is the realization of the quest for an efficient means for human interaction. The environment then becomes more than a locational expression; it is, in its structured processes, an intricate communications system upon which urbanites rely for the satisfaction of the interdependencies crucial to their existence. The functional interdependencies activate a complexity of linking interactions as expressed by spatial configurations of the communications, transportation, and activities networks. The emergence of a fecundity of interaction considerations concretizes the idea of urban communities as functional processes.

The discussion of the urban environment has, thus far, been confined to the system's "spatial structure." The "physical" composition of the structure is formed by a miscellany of buildings, streets, and other man-made artifacts, and is expressed as the "geophysical base for community life."[1] The introduction of the consideration of "functional processes" validates interaction analysis as germane to the spatial patterning of urban activity. However, both processes have been framed in the context of a spatial matrix concerned with the distribution of people, physical objects, and activities within delineated space. There has been no conceptual dichotomy between the physical environment and the activity systems as they remained conceptually mutually accommodative. But a holistic scrutiny of the interacting networks of

[1] Donald L. Foley, "An Approach to Metropolitan Spatial Structure," in Melvin M. Webber, *et al., Explorations into Urban Structure* (Philadelphia: University of Pennsylvania Press, 1964).

functional processes in the contemporary era finds the activity systems transcending spatial regions to fashion an "urban realm."[2]

The urban realm is not tied to concepts of territorial specificity, but is the manifestation of functional processes through space. It is the outgrowth of modern technology, communications, and institutional changes, coupled with transnational mobility and expanded specialization, which have made imperative activities beyond place-communities. The urban realm has affected the Euclidean context of spatiality of stable physical locational patterns; it is the sum of activity patterns in terms of an afocal process of human interactions subject to continuous variation and ambiguity.

The concept of the urban realm emphasizes the dependence of urban regions upon the activity processes—technological, economic, social and political—of the greater environment. The physical and activity patterns within the regions are subject to decisions and policies of national corporations, the national government, a national financial system, and other "non-place" institutions in the urban realm. Realistically, the afocality of the urban system will undoubtedly increase, as the dynamism of urban life causes interactions to be marked by more diffusion and aspatiality and by less attachment to the nodal community.

Thus, the urban system is modeled in terms of three dimensions of ascending activity complexity. Dimension 1 is concerned with the physical plant, equipment and resources, and territorial boundaries within the system. It is spatially fixed within a delimited urban region and consists of discrete political settlements of varying intensities of urbanness. The physical spatial dimension is microscopically oriented to the communities-as-entities which form a limited-region system.

Dimension 2 exceeds the spatially determinate physical perspective by its consideration of activity interaction, albeit within a circumscribed physical environment. Here the func-

---

[2] Melvin M. Webber, "The Urban Place and the Nonplace Urban Realms," in Webber, *et al., op. cit.*

tional processes transcend discrete politically demarcated territorial units in pursuit of definable activity linkages within the
system. Activity flows are perceived as the causality and the
controlling device of their physical environment.

Dimension 3 is a holistic system-subsystem macro-analysis
of all human interactions. It relates to the linkages among
myriad interacting activities forming the spatially unlimited
network of functional interdependencies.

While the trichotomy may deceptively appear dis-
harmonious to the system's integrity, the dimensions, as distinct components, fulfill the requisite of differentiation, and as
interacting variables, are functionally integrated within the
system. Dimension 3's aspect is the afocal macro-functional
flows of people, goods, information, and money; dimension 2's
concern is with the allocation of activities and activity places
within a defined region; and, dimension 1 pertains to the
locations of the physical plants which house the activities, and
the people who perform them. Accordingly, the three dimensions are overtly linked by their discrete engagement with the
interdependent and interacting variables of physical plant, activity locations, and human interactions. Hence, the urban
environment is a functioning system composed of the three
interacting dimensions.

The essence of the political system is "making authoritative decisions that allocate advantages and disadvantages for an
entire society."[3] In support of this, the system must muster
the consent of its constituents in the social environment to
create a legitimacy for its structures and functions. In turn,
legitimacy is predicated upon the system's contributions to the
social environment. Thus, implicit to the existence of the
system is the mobilization of resources to maintain its viability
and to achieve its goals. The interaction between the system
and the environment is the means by which the political
processes contribute to system persistence.

The political system maintains a constant interchange

[3] Stephen V. Monsma, *American Politics, A Systems Approach*
(New York: Holt, Rinehart and Winston, Inc., 1969), p. 9; Easton,
op. cit

with the environment by means of a feedback loop consisting of outputs, inputs, and feedback. The outputs, authoritative decisions, are in the form of applications or interpretations of rules, which have an effect on the environment. The environment's inputs consist of support—either passive acquiescence or active voting, speaking, and writing; demands as articulated through interest-representation processes—by individuals, interest groups, political parties, communications media—or extraordinarily exhibited by demonstrations, strikes, and insofar as extralegal manifestations; expectations—the latent demands for culturally conforming behavior among political actors; and, feedback, which is the measure of the social environment's satisfaction with the political system's outputs. The system, for its persistence, is keyed to continued support from the environment, as manifested by feedback loop inputs.[4]

There is, in the system persistence process, a duality of orientation. On the one hand, the system and its actors, must be sensitive to problems perceived in the environment that may call for changes in substantive goals; while, on the other hand, a commitment to the status quo, in the face of potential strain induced by goal redirection, may impel a reticence for problem-solving. The tension is between the structure-changing features in adaptation to the physical and social environment, and structure-maintaining tendencies. The system's necessary adherence to its persistence allows for this internal symbiosis and seeks to abate this tension through conflict minimization and compromise. Without the reconciliation of conflicting demands and expectations, the system would become immobilized and, correspondingly, fail to provide adequately for environmental exigencies.

The disparities in the system persistence process are characterized by the contradictory orientations of structure-maintaining and adaptive processes and actors. Structure-maintaining exigencies are effected by the use of legitimacy creating normative and prescriptive tenets of societal values, symbols and ideologies. Conflict resolution and environmental

---

[4] Easton, *op. cit.;* Monsma, *op. cit.*

support are inherent to the political system's perpetuity, and the structure maintaining processes are focused on system stability and homeostatic equilibrium. Adaptive functions, conversely, are sensitized to environmental problems and demands even though these may transcend the general value schemes of the system. This is not to say that the adaptive perspective is occlusive to system persistence, or that system equilibrium is contingent upon an enduring primacy of normative goal-directed actors and processes. A political system without the means or the inclination to adapt to the demands of the external environment, nor the acuity to convert these inputs into appropriate outputs, condemns itself to entropy. Historically the system then flounders in a state of anesthetized incompetence and inertness, gradually—or suddenly—subjected to increasing disorders in the social environment. Ultimately the system may cease to persist in its existing state as its legitimacy is wrested by legal or extralegal forces in the environment.

At the heart of a political system's functional processes is the animus for the stability and the survival of the system. But the system's persistence is not locked to immutable *a priori* goals. It is the system's outputs which stimulate the environment's feedback, conditioning its support for the system. Thus, the system's endurance is reliant upon the interactions of its functionally interdependent variables and their interaction with the external environment. There need not be, in a dynamic and goal-seeking political system, an irreconcilable dichotomy between the system's normative demands and its demands for adaptation to the processes of change. It is the very interaction of normative and prescriptive demands with the adaptive exactions which furnishes the system with an equilibrium seeking paradigm in a morphogenic, cybernetics sense. In this manner, the system is less likely to be seduced by expedient panaceas or routinized into obstinate rigidity.

The model of a political system is that of an organic unity made up of a hierarchy of differentiated and integrated subsystems, with the units of each level of complexity composed of a variety of units from the next subordinate level, down to the basic unit of the individual acting in a political role. The

analogy is particularly germane to the American political
system which is disposed toward functional specialization,
with subfunctions distributed among participating subsystems.
Government, in the systemic context, is located within the
political system and is allocated the responsibility for formal
decision making. It is through government that interest articulated demands are converted into policy outputs. The policy
flow to the environment is in the form of rules which are sub-
stantively differentiated and performed by diversified subsystems. Operationally, the application of rules are dispersed
so that the

> . . . congressional subsystem is primarily involved in
> rule initiation, the administrative subsystems are primarily
> involved in rule application, the judicial subsystem is pri-
> marily involved in rule interpretation, and the presiden-
> tial subsystem is involved in all three. Interest representa-
> tion goes on throughout the major subsystems and by
> means of semiofficial and unofficial channels of communi-
> cation.[5]

The American political culture of "checks and balances"
and "separation of powers," coupled with the diffusive and
devolutionary qualities of federalism, has borne not only an
energetic interaction between the system and the environment,
but has compelled an equally animated intercourse within the
system. Subsystem intercourse proceeds both horizontally and
vertically among the levels of the federalist structure. Support
is generated through a feedback flow, with each level expending
its ration of outputs, support, expectations and demands. Thus
the political system is a complex multiplicity of interdependent
units incessantly interacting with the external environment
and with one another. The conversion processes are subject
to myriad conflicting pressures often resulting in unsustained
and cannibalized outputs flows, hence giving rise to the
characterization of a democratic political system, operant in a
large and heterogeneous society, as a process distinguished by
its stasis. The challenge of the system has never been more
urgent, now that the acceleration of history has propelled the

[5] Monsma, *op. cit.,* p. 15.

complexities of the environment beyond the reaches of static institutions.

The Linkage of the Systems

The planning process, an administrative subsystem, is an adaptive function *vis a vis* its environment. It is for this analysis, the key linkage between the urban and the political systems because in its functional responsibility to effectuate an ordered development of human settlements, it can provide a coherence to the articulation of the complexities of interacting urban variables and the analogous decision-making process.

Symptomatic of urban and metropolitan planning has been the "unitary" bias of comprehending urban communities in terms of graphic replications of the spatial, physical environment.[6] Consistently, the planning activity, operating within this conceptual framework, has sought the disposition of physical patterns in a congruity with a scheme for a future ideal. Implicit in this is confidence in the inducement of designated processes of human interaction by the manipulation of spatial arrangements. In this manner, planning has been utilized as an instrument of control over physical organization for the encouragement of a selected development pattern. Crucial to its distinction, too, is the unitary approach's commitment to a microanalytic treatment of discrete planning units. Founded upon intuition and synthesis, this approach treats entities as unique and self-sufficient. This is transferred, in application, to a design context of dealing with individual communities as autonomous wholes, conceived as possessing a sense of social unity, in addition to a geophysical integrity.

The selected development pattern is thus formalized by a considerably detailed optative statement of goals in terms of form and size to be reached at a given point in time by the unit in consideration. The "goal" plan commonly known as a "general" or a "comprehensive" plan, is typically a manuscript of graphic statements—including a written text, charts, maps,

[6] Foley in Webber, *et al., op. cit.*

and drawings—proffering a two-dimensional model of spatial cultivation. Because of its emphasis upon the arrangements of the kind and place of the major land usages, transportation networks, and physical plants, goal planning has been appropriate at both the local and metropolitan levels.

Eminently useful at the spatial-physical level of comprehension, unitary goal planning has been remiss in its treatment of the functional expressions in the urban environment. The consideration of the large dimensions of the urban system, with a focus upon the functional interdependencies contained therein, requires a macroscopic frame of analysis. The analysis must transcend the determinate particularization of the urban spatial form in "place" terms, by the supplemental examination of activities as spatially constituted courses of human interaction.

A macroanalytic planning focus is an exploration of the various functionally interdependent parts, interacting over time and space, integrated within the urban system. This is an "organic" orientation which allows that the urban system is a functionally cohesive whole and is made up of its interdependent and interacting constituent units, or subsystems. Functionally, the organic planning process seeks to obtain knowledge of how the myriad actors—persons, households, firms, governments—interact, and how this affects urban area development over time. This planning approach is a product of the interdependence and pluralism of government, producer, and consumer actions, as a natural consequence of an ever greater intensification of specialization and division of labor, and interchange of effort. The organic concept of planning, by its analytic preoccupation with the discernment of functional-relations and form-relations, can discriminate among the physical pattern, spatial activity, and spatial interaction linkages, for a correlative development process.

The organic process's formulation of a plan would resemble a goal plan only insofar as it could result in a publicized document. Regarding a posture outlining a detailed program for a future locational form as dysfunctional, this planning method would seek to influence the apposite development processes to the desirable criteria. This is founded upon the concern for the environment's dynamic ambiguity and continuous variation, which requires a strategem for adaptation to the impelling changes. Accordingly, static goals for a physical order would be supplanted by a "strategic" plan of alternative development expediencies with an evaluation of predicted consequences of each upon the preferred criteria of conditions. Planning, in this sense, would be the devising of a strategy to bring about conditions within its locality and in the interdependent environment, which are consistent with the realization of objectives. This would intend the manipulation of those governmental and market processes and locational preferences linked to the cause of development. Strategic planning, therefore, is the framing of functional and processual objectives for an ordered development, and the substantive actualization of these objectives.

The efficacy of organic planning is that, by using systems analysis, it may come to grips with the most obdurate problems of the urban environment, many of them, such as overpopulation, transportation, pollution, and housing, are joined in physical, social, economic and political interdependence. The organic systems planning process, by viewing the miscellany of variables as morphological is dependent upon an uninterrupted flow of related information from these sources for coherent managerial deduction. Delays, distortions, or breakages in the lines of communication to decision points negate the leverage afforded by such a process. "Method, order, and arrangement for program accomplishment characterize a systems approach."[7] Information is instrumental to the success of system control.

When each of the subsystems of the community has complete information about itself, about its alternatives

[7] Herman G. Berkman, "The Scope of Scientific Technique and Information Technology in Metropolitan Area Analysis," in Stephen B. Sweeney and James C. Charlesworth, *Governing Urban Society: New Scientific Approaches,* Monograph 7 (Philadelphia: The American Academy of Political and Social Science, May, 1967), pp. 170–171.

and the effects of these alternatives for itself and for the other subsystems (which are mutually affecting one another), it is in a better position to decide and to act, and in the process of so doing naturally effects better control and utilization of community resources.[8]

Systems planning, through information management under proper feedback control, can be the mechanism through which a community (or a region and perhaps the urban realm) becomes a self-controlling cybernetic system with regard to its development. Fundamental to a control system is that the network of information flow through a medium of control. As the medium, a planning information system becomes the key to a self-controlling system's ability to adapt itself to its environment or to modulate the environment for its needs. Information is not only indispensable for a cybernetic regulation process but it is also essential for a rational plan-decision making. Rational decision making consists of receiving information, processing it, and acting upon the process outcome in some meaningful way. A planning information system, unless integrated, labors under a handicap of functional constriction, and could become a focus of controversy and detraction as results inevitably fall short of expectations.

Urban systems management, to be operationally feasible, must realize access across jurisdictional and functional lines, to the extent of the interdependence of information requirements, for the utilization of functionally integrating horizontal and vertical systems analysis. The linkage of vertical systems, the process of integrating a specific function through the several levels of government, with horizontal systems, the process integrating differentiated interacting functions across political jurisdictions, is the means by which data become relevant to a unit of analysis. By such linkages, a unit can be

[8] Kenneth L. Kraemer, "The Planning Subsystem #9," *A Municipal Information and Decision System,* Vol. II, *Vertical Subsystems,* Carl F. Davis, Jr. (ed.) (Los Angeles: Municipal Systems Research, University of Southern California, School of Public Administration, 1968), p. 13.

examined for its impact upon the system and with the assurance that interdependencies have been included.[9]

While the frame of reference for information systems has been that of a public information system intended for the attainment of community self regulation and rational public decision making, information, or the lack of it, also bears a major impact on market forces. A governing factor of urban growth and development is the dependency upon the allocation of market resources based upon market decisions. The determinants of market behavior are various and it is not uncommon for the market to operate on premises unsubstantiated by fact or with contentions replete with inaccuracies. Market decisions are therefore predicated upon intuitive judgments of the decision makers and the lure of locational attractions judged by such factors as general public policies, tax structures, and social and aesthetic conditions. The availability of a comprehensive data system would be of value to both public and private decision making, particularly in view of their interdependence.

> Systems analysis, then, is a technique for scientific application of information made available through advance data processing and communications technologies. In addition, it lends itself to the intelligent establishment of weighing of alternative goals, in terms of the resources to be devoted to their attainment.[10]

The scientific application of information intends an integrated information system enlisting the cooperation and participation of urban communities and whole regions. This

[9] "Most problems within the urban area, such as those involving transportation, waste disposal, and land management, can be adequately solved only on a metropolitan basis. Metropolitan transportation studies, for example, focus on the total urban area and must assemble data for the total urban area." Joel M. Kibbee, "The Scope of Large-Scale Computer-Based Systems in Governmental Functions," in Sweeney and Charlesworth, *op. cit.,* p. 191.

[10] John Diebold, "Impacts on Urban Governmental Functions of Developments in Science and Technology," in Sweeney and Charlesworth, *op. cit.,* p. 89.

would mean that the units in the communications network must acquire internal technical facilities and competence to sustain a flow of compatible data for the computerized information system. The development of a computerized technology for individual units, in addition to providing a linkage to the system's network, grants an autonomy for defining information utilities for local resources and uses.

The advent of applied technology for improved planning and programming ultimately assumes institutional arrangements capable of coping with this development. The management of urban resources, utilizing the full scope of the systems analysis process, posits a phasing-out of incompatible institutions to be replaced by those capable of adapting to a changing environment and of objectifying the options offered by science and technology.

Technology's "hardware"—the machines, instruments, and materials—are no more than the implements by which man seeks an understanding of the intricacies of nature. It is the managers of our society who must have the ability to prepare the programs suited for the machines' comprehension, and then relate their attendant revelations to the needs of man. The competency required for control of the manifestations of information technology, the "software" of the process, necessitates a revolution in the art and science of management. A total systems approach by planning, aided by information-processing, electronic data-processing, network analysis, and other quantifiable techniques, makes it suited to an interdisciplinary synthesis for problem solving, and a management science which affirms the furnishing of timely and accurate comprehensive information to decision makers.

The prospect for modeling an urban system, a feat as yet unaccomplished even to the extent of fashioning a useful city "systems model," would be the function of "systems engineering," a management science prodigy. Systems engineering, at its most ambitious,

> . . . would examine the city in the round as a total
> systems complex, inter-relating all its demographic, eco-
> nomic, social and physical components, with a view to

arriving at more integrated solutions to the multiple problems.[11]

The task would enlist a broad spectrum of disciplines, and include such experts as economists, physicists, ecologists, sociologists, mathematicians, political scientists, and meteorologists, all interactant with systems engineers as "idea brokers." This multifarious endeavor points to the exaction of a full array of alternative solutions to problems with concomitant evaluations of their costs and benefits as the surest route to optimum decision making.

At the simplest level, systems engineering is just logical, common sense planning, not remarkably different from the procedure followed in other disciplinary pursuits. At its most sophisticated, it is an uncommon, intricately organized method for bringing to bear all relevant scientific, technical, and other resources upon the analysis and systematic solution of complex problems. In the process, it employs such mathematical tools as input-output techniques, linear and non-linear programming, cost-effectiveness formulas, simulation modeling, feedback theory, queuing theory, and other esoteric techniques transposed from the physical sciences.[12]

Systems engineering's functional course, preceding the decision making point, is generally typical of the systems planning form. During the basic, or systems exploratory, planning phase, a problem is defined and the limits of the system are determined. Then, all of the appropriate information on the "structured" system and its environment is analyzed and screened for the purpose of providing a narrowed field of feasible alternatives. These undergo further purging, under scrutiny, until only the best possible solutions survive. The ultimate managerial decision of the selection of the best course and its subsequent implementation, is retained by the political institution employing the systems engineers. Thus, the confluence of all planning activity is at the policy making

[11] Lawrence Lessing, "Systems Engineering Invades the City," *Fortune,* Vol. 77, No. 1 (January, 1968), p. 156.
[12] *Ibid.,* pp. 156–157.

point, and without a directive authorizing product implementation, the planning process is tantamount to a didactic exercise.

Planning and the Political System

There is no doubt that management science has supported institutions charged with the authority of alleviating urban problems with an increased decision making rationality, by making available a cohesive breadth of information and data, along with problem-solving alternatives. Yet, despite the acceleration of computer capability and proven resourcefulness, there has been limited call for its application, as "the initial payoff in information systems for functional areas of government is still primarily in the automation of routine tasks."[13]

In contrast to the case of the monolithic aerospace industry, where systems analysis is well regarded, there is a contrariness to this process in the highly fragmented public sector. The unresponsiveness of governments to systems management may perhaps be keyed to an essential tension between societal goals and orientations and those of the systems approach. A holistic planning orientation perceives itself in terms of a functional, efficient service for an organismic society. Society, however, is the sum of the aggregation of its component units, and the basic element, the individual, does not necessarily operate in terms of logic and rationality. Individuals, even when political actors are often swayed by emotion, prejudices, and cultural dogmas.

> Management science techniques can give us basic data on where to bus, on the costs of busing—and on the quantitative, short-run, learning results from such a step. But the values and emotions of both Negroes and whites are not, and will not be for a long time, if ever, subject to a strict cost benefit analysis. Again, values, prejudices, and emotions are paramount.[14]

[13] Kibbee, *op. cit.,* p. 184.

[14] Matthias E. Lukens, "Emerging Executive and Organizational Responses to Scientific and Technological Developments," in Sweeney and Charlesworth, *op. cit.,* p. 120.

Demonstrations of rational decision making through greater governmental coordination, coupled with the uses of comprehensive computer based data accumulation and analysis processes, may elicit a scenario of Gothic oppression. Often, "good" government holds sway over "efficient" government. Many citizens prefer a government that provides a "reasonable level of services" and affords individuals ample opportunity for access and representation, to an "efficient" government characterized as a dehumanized behemoth. Accordingly, systems planning's acceptability is subject to continued controversy so long as it is functionally at variance with widely accepted norms, standards, and attitudes. The dearth of comprehensive systems utilization in government can be attributed to decision makers' responsiveness to the demand inputs of the political environment.

> In the long run . . . it seems likely that we must establish a more fruitful and more informed dialogue between the custodians of social value and the custodians of scientific and technological expertise. In the dialogue, the politicians, the social scientists, and the humanists must become more knowledgeable as to the technological means that are or may become available for achieving social ends, while the technologist must attempt to understand more adequately the total social matrix in which his inventions are embedded and which they both serve and modify.[15]

Management science is used by governments as a means to an end, for decision making remains a human process, and particularly so in the highly charged political environment. Often assailed by a plethora of conflicting and differentiated demands, the political policy maker must often fall back upon his experience and intuitive judgment for the assignment of problem priorities and the allocation of available resources to such problems. This is sometimes done by well intentioned

[15] Britton Harris, "Transportation and Urban Goals," *Science, Engineering, and the City,* A Symposium sponsored jointly by the National Academy of Sciences and the National Academy of Engineering (Washington, D.C.: National Academy of Sciences, Publication 1498, 1967), p. 36.

instinctive rationality for the common good; and sometimes as an adaptation to demand realities, or in a submission to political expediency.

Public decisions are reached through a complex of public and private agents, through a network of communication, accommodation, and agreement, which is always open to change if sufficient influence can be mobilized, if facts can be presented, if choices can be made clear, and the consequences of choices for particular interest-groups can be brought home to those groups.[16]

In view of the dynamics of the political system, planning must contend with a host of heterogeneous rivals for the favorable attention of the policy making process. This actuality compels planners to become dexterous political actors with an acuity for anticipating the behavior of other actors. Planning alternatives and systems studies must be conceptualized in the context of understood assumptions about human actions. While this may appear as self-evident, the systems technique, inured to the less capricious hardware systems of weapons and aerospace, will find this feature of a social system a challenge to its scientific ingenuity. Planners, as actors, may have to abjure the modeling process in terms of quantifying the human condition at the policy making level, and join in this social system armed only with their own perceptivity. Should planning fail to adapt to these circumstances within the political environment it would then become functionally impotent and thereby reduced to a bureaucratic sloth without any conjunctive value to the urban and political systems. Implicitly, the same consequences would befall the planning function should the political system unilaterally quarantine it from the decision-making processes. This would suggest the need for active reciprocity in the interaction between government and planning, insofar as energizing the latter's political and functional perspicacity and impact.

In connection with its functionally conjuctive aspect,

[16] William L. C. Wheaton, "Public and Private Agents of Change in Urban Expansion," in Webber, *et al., op. cit ,* p. 188.

another planning task is to cohere and articulate the many and differentiated policy outputs appropriate to urban systems development, originating at numerous governmental agencies and levels. Characteristic of the American polity is the proliferation of functional rules, treating the identical subject in a different light according to the agency of issuance. As in the process of the ordering of informational systems flow to decision makers, is the analogous need for a disciplined control of the feedback flow output. With this in mind, planners can play a vital role in educating policy makers to an appreciation of the value for rule consistency, and in the process, correspondingly influence policy. The merits of this avocation are certain to be reflected in the feedback from the *cognoscente* of the well-served systems.

The planning process's interaction with variables within the two systems, and an intersystem causal interdependence of these interactions evidences a role of functional linkage. Requisite to an effective performance of intersystem integration, however, is the link's effectiveness in finding an equilibrium between normative and dynamic systemic adaptation demands. That is to say, planning's intersystem conjunctive aspect is predicated upon its efficacy in adapting to both systems—in normative and mechanistic terms—and in integrating its internal processes.

II

Urbanization and
Its Discontents

Growth of the City

C ONTEMPORARY CIVILIZATION is marked by high-density population centers in spatially limited areas—clusters of people, businesses, activities, and interactions forming the "urban environment." Detractors of this development perceive it as consisting of monotonous sprawls of endless "ticky-tack" suburbs surrounding spent and sterile central cities. The quality of city life is seen as degraded by the perpetual stresses of noise and pollution, incoherent architecture, and amorphous multitudes and institutions.[1] This city stunts individuals by hindering their interchange with their environment, leading to mass rootlessness and alienation.[2]

The city's decay is marked by the persistent exodus of leadership and tax-paying middle and high-income groups with

[1] Kevin Lynch, "The City as Environment," in *Cities,* A Scientific American Book (New York: Alfred A. Knopf, 1969).

[2] William Kornhauser, *The Politics of Mass Society,* The Free Press of Glencoe (Illinois, 1959).

this void being filled by low income and low leadership-potential minorities, resulting in debilitated tax structures and sociological upheavals.[3] The suburbs where the middle and high-income families move, are not immune from criticism. Suburban dwellers are often depicted as "petty bourgeois in status and prejudice" living insular lives apart from the more diverse culture of the city and even from their wage-earners.[4] The aesthetics of suburban developments, too, are noteworthy of criticism:

> Spaced throughout the suburban grid are likely to be small developments of private real estate men, attempting a more picturesque arrangement of the plots. But on the whole the pressure for profit is such that the plots become minimal and the endless rows of little boxes, or of larger boxes with picture windows, are pretty near the landscape of Dante's first volume.[5]

Urban development in history[6] can be traced from the preindustrial medieval cities which functioned primarily as governmental and religious centers with commerce as an ancillary. The industrializing city, next in historic progression, evolved away from traditional societal forms and mores and saw the emergence of the economic-technological order. The industrial city, a product of the Industrial Revolution, grew out of the specialized division of labor required by the developing technology, and this division of labor, coupled with increased productivity allowed for a high population concentration in the cities. The diversity of the city's goods and services was made possible by bringing together workers and

[3] Calvin S. Hamilton, "The Role of Local Government in the Urban Crisis," *Urban America: Crisis and Opportunity,* Jim Chard and Jon York eds. (Belmont, Calif.: Dickenson Publ. Co., 1969).

[4] Percival and Paul Goodman, *Communitas, Means of Livelihood and Ways of Life* (New York: Vintage Books, 1960).

[5] *Ibid.,* p. 28.

[6] Gideon Sjoberg, "Cities in Developing and Industrial Societies; A Comparative Sociological Approach," *Taming Megalopolis,* Vol. 1, *What Is and What Could Be,* H. Wentworth Eldredge (ed.) (Garden City, N.Y.: Anchor Books, Doubleday & Co., Inc., 1967).

entrepreneurs of diverse skills and needs.[7] The early industrial city's population movement was a centripetal rural migration that provided the labor force. As modes of transportation became mechanized a small centrifugal movement in the city fringes—"streetcar suburbs"—occurred. The advent of electric commuter railroads, high-speed buses, and private motor vehicles caused a larger centrifugal flow to the suburbs extending urbanism to metropolitan dimensions culminating in the present-day sprawling pattern of high-density clusters.[8]

City Becomes Metropolis

The Federal Government first accorded official recognition to metropolitan areas in 1910. To facilitate the analysis of metropolitan problems the Standard Metropolitan Area became the areal criterion in 1949, to provide all federal statistical agencies with the same geographical boundaries in collecting and publishing data. The current nomenclature of "Standard Metropolitan Statistical Area" (SMSA) is descriptive of a contiguous area of economic and social interdependencies, albeit retaining a series of autonomous political jurisdictions.[9]

The definition of an individual SMSA involves two considerations: first, a city or cities of specified population to constitute the central city and to identify the county in which it is located as the central county; and, second, economic and social relationships with contiguous[10] counties which are metropolitan in character, so that the periphery

[7] Hans Blumenfeld, "The Human Metropolis," in *Cities, op. cit.*
[8] H. Wentworth Eldredge, "Peoples Urbanization and City Growth," in Eldredge, Vol. 1, *op cit.*
[9] U.S. Census Bureau, 18th Census, 1960, U.S. Census of Population, Standard Metropolitan Statistical Areas (Washington, D.C.); Joseph F. Zimmerman (ed.), 1968 *Metropolitan Area Annual* (Albany, N.Y.: Graduate School of Public Affairs, State University of New York at Albany, 1968).
[10] "A 'contiguous' county either adjoins the county or counties containing the largest city in the area, or adjoins an intermediate county integrated with the central county. There is no limit to the number of tiers of outlying metropolitan counties so long as all other criteria are met " U.S. Census, *Ibid.*, p. viii.

of the specified metropolitan area may be determined. SMSA's may cross State lines.[11]

Population criteria are that the standard statistical area must include a city with a population of 50,000 or more, or two contiguous cities constituting a single community because of social and economic ties, having a combined minimum population of 50,000, with the smaller city possessing at least 15,000 inhabitants. The requirement for an area to qualify as metropolitan in character is that the county be a place of work of a labor force of which at least 75 percent is non-agricultural, and a place of residence for a dense pattern of contiguous settlement.[12] Additionally, a degree of social and economic interdependence between the central county and its environs must be manifested by proximate living and employment locations.[13] Two hundred sixty-seven Standard Metropolitan Statistical Areas, ranging in population from 51,000 to 11 million, are located in every state of the Union, except Alaska, Wyoming and Vermont, and are generally named after the area's principal city.[14]

The federal government's accordance of metropolitan recognition to 267 areas in the United States is in response to the growing awareness of the development of high-density, spatially-concentrated, and market and culturally induced population clusters. The proliferation of contiguous areas of compact settlements, interdependent economically and socially and sharing fundamental problems, has become the post-industrial urban pattern.[15] The communality in the form and functioning of large urban areas attests to the incipient urban pattern which can be generalized as typical.

[11] *Ibid.*, p. viii.

[12] "It must have 50 percent or more of its population living in contiguous minor civil divisions with a density of at least 150 persons per square mile, in an unbroken chain of minor civil divisions wth such density radiating from a central city in the area." *Ibid.*

[13] *Ibid.*

[14] Letter from Advisory Commission on Intergovernmental Relations, Washington, D.C., March 8, 1972.

[15] Benjamin Chinitz, "New York: A Metropolitan Region," in *Cities, op. cit.*

The contemporary model of urban development has been caused by the changes in forms of production and consumption and by the proliferation of new modes of transportation.[16] The metropolis, advantaged by its compact market, offers workers, employers, and consumers great breadth of choice of goods and services, in addition to being indispensably linked to the efficacy of business enterprises.

Only a metropolis can support the large inventories, transportation facilities, and specialized services—particularly those of a financial, legal, technical and promotional nature—that are essential to modern business.[17]

Compact market areas are products of modern technology whereby the dependence of manufacturing on raw materials has been supplanted by a need for manufacturing interdependence requiring market proximity. Earlier industrial manufacturing, because of transportation limitations, clustered in cities, particularly near railroads and waterways. The development of new modes of transport and efficient highways has freed manufacturing from fixed lines of transportation and allowed a wider areal dispersion, from city to metropolitan proportions. Accordingly, the spatial dispersion of commerce and population in urban areas was influenced by contemporary transportation patterns and networks. Substantial increases of transportation capabilities resulting in the more efficient movement of people and goods has permitted the existing pattern of dispersed settlement and its accompanying service and manufacturing industries.

Although it has been attributed that the automobile has been the cause of urban decentralization, economic variables have also been causal to the shift of people and goods.[18] Industry's move to the city's environs followed the necessities of modern production techniques requiring large tracts of land

[16] Benjamin Chinitz, "Introduction," *City and Suburb, the Economics of Metropolitan Growth*, Chinitz (ed.) (Englewood Cliffs, N.J.: Prentice-Hall, Inc., 1964).

[17] Blumenfeld, in *Cities, op. cit.*, p. 45.

[18] John R. Meyer, "Knocking Down the Strawmen," Chinitz (ed.), *op. cit.*

to house extensive one-story manufacturing layouts, instead of the traditional several story factories in clustered surroundings.[19] Additionally, trucking, "piggybacking" and other new freight moving techniques have obviated the need for centralized locations; and the economies in warehousing and freight handling for retail industries in the peripheries are substantial. The emerging commercial pattern in urban areas is that the central business district is losing its manufacturing, retailing, household services, and wholesaling to the suburbs, while gaining in service industries—banks, law firms, advertising agencies, financial brokerages, management consultants, government agencies, and the like.[20]

Despite the occurrence of urban decentralization and the shift of several traditional city functions to the outlying areas, this does not necessarily signal the demise of the central city. Increases in the standard of living and of the educational level of the general public have given rise to a sophistication which seeks the luxuries, diversity, and attractions of downtown.[21] The present era of urban development—the post-industrial city—is characterized by industries, employees, and the non-job oriented population seeking out new amenities, giving impetus to even greater diversity and resources.[22] The rise of suburbanization is balanced by increasing managerial activities in the city's core as witnessed by the proliferation of sky-

[19] The automobile, however, is also a factor in the need for broader land tracts and less-clustered surroundings. Large parking lots are now needed for the employee's private vehicles, and central city clustering and heavy vehicular traffic are impediments to the efficient flow of goods and the required manufacturing transportation system.

[20] Benjamin Chinitz, Chinitz (ed.), *op. cit*

[21] William Alonso, "Cities and City Planners," *Taming Megalopolis,* Vol. II, *How to Manage an Urbanized World,* H. Wentworth Eldredge (ed.) (Garden City, N.Y.: Anchor Books, Doubleday & Co., Inc., 1967).

[22] Wilfred Owen, "Transport: Key to the Future of Cities," *The Quality of the Urban Environment, Essays on 'New Resources' in An Urban Age,* Harvey S. Perloff (ed.) (published by Resources for the Future, Inc., distributed by the Johns Hopkins Press, Baltimore, Md., 1969).

scrapers on the city's skyline. The skyscraper—"an expression of the social evolution of employment, of the labor force to-day"[23]—is the manifestation of the influx of white collar labor as the major urban capital sector of economic activity as well as the mark of high-rise luxury apartment construction. The city houses many schools of higher learning, and many scientific and research centers, in addition to providing a myriad of modern leisure-time pursuits.[24]

The disadvantage in the shift of the city's economic activities from manufacturing to managerial services lies in the creation of a class of urban unemployables. Manufacturing and wholesaling industries, traditional employers of low-skilled workers, have relocated to the environs, leaving the central city slum dwellers, predominantly Negroes, without opportunity for employment.[25] The core city's prospering service industries require the performance of skilled and literate tasks for which the slum dwellers are unsuited, and this minimization of their employment results in heavy fiscal costs to the city in the form of welfare payments, tax roll losses, and expenditures for service in a highly volatile social environment.

> . . . A new class has emerged in the urban labor market. Its members are separated from the mainstream of economic activity by deficiencies in skill and education, pronounced gaps in the labor market information system, and increased physical distance.[26]

The prosperity of the metropolitan area is dependent upon its economic specialization and trade with the outside world. For an area to develop it must compete effectively with other areas. An expanding area's economic sector will pay higher wages, thereby attracting a more skilled pool of labor, and adding to the overall prosperity. It is expected that an urban area will pay high incomes when its economy (1) uses

[23] Jean Gottmann, "Why the Skyscraper," Eldredge, Vol. I, *op. cit.*
[24] Gideon Sjoberg, "The City in Twentieth Century America," Chard and York (eds.), *op. cit.*
[25] Chinitz in Chinitz (ed.), *op. cit.*
[26] Arnold R. Weber, "Labor Market Perspectives of the New City," Chinitz (ed.), *op. cit*, p. 74.

relatively high proportions of the more skilled occupations, (2) has high capital-to-labor ratios, and (3) sells in oligopolistic markets.[27] The key to expansion is a circular formula: a diversified industrial structure serves as the catalyst for economic advantages; yet industry mix begets more mix because of reliance upon economic interdependence. An area with an industrial cluster has more appeal than an area without one, because of the presence of a competent labor force and a wide variety in the service sector.[28] But, the presence of a competent labor force, and an efficient service sector are tied to an expanding economic structure. This is the reason why established urban areas, such as New York City, Los Angeles, and San Francisco, retain and attract new industries more readily than developing or stagnant areas. The attraction of new industry is related to those areas' population growths.

> The nature of an area's labor market, the cost and availability of land within its boundaries, its relation to the nation's everchanging transportation network, the tax structure and financing possibilities it offers to new enterprises, and the degree to which it is able to offer services and facilities important to new manufacturing establishments—all these factors and many more help to determine a metropolitan area's advantage or disadvantage in holding its share of a particular industry or attracting a larger one.[29]

The pattern of income distribution has a powerful effect on the form and functioning of the city and, paradoxically, affluence as well as poverty is costly to urban government.[30] Affluence leads to more private vehicles which cause traffic congestion, smog, and a demand for greater land space. Proliferation of industries and population adds to the pollution problem. Haphazard and indifferent growth patterns have underlined the urban miseries so that

[27] Wilbur R. Thompson, "Urban Economics," in Eldredge, Vol. I, *op. cit.,* p. 160.

[28] Chinitz in Chinitz (ed.), *op. cit.,* p. 18.

[29] *Ibid.*

[30] Thompson in Eldredge (ed.), Vol. I, *op. cit.*

The positive appeal of the modern city—the stimulating pageant of diversity, the opportunities for intellectual growth, the new freedom for individuality—have been
increasingly affected by the overwhelming social and economic engineering problems that have been the by-product
of poorly planned growth . . . .
. . . Even the flight to the suburb—in part a protest
against the erosion of the urban milieu—has had its element of irony, for the exodus has intensified our reliance
on the automobile, and the freeway as indispensable elements of modern life. More often than not, the suburban-
ite's quest for open space and serenity has been defeated by
the processes of pell-mell growth.[31]

Large urban areas have in common the manufacturing
concentration within their industrial sectors, a similar pattern
of income distribution, population pressure, and the need for a
spatial pattern of the local public economy. Manufacturing
interdependency rationally produces industrial clustering, giving momentum for even more cluster in an effort to maximize
internal and external economies. The pattern and divergence
in income distribution have unstable effects upon the urban
form, as poverty produces a debilitating effect upon residents
and their locale of residence, with concomitant deprivation to
a community's competitive posture for private investment and
development. Affluence, which generates even more affluence
and increasing consumption demands for greater amenities,
optimizes industrial output.

Accelerated industrial productivity maximizes its efficiency by emphasizing a diminishing per-unit cost-ratio through
economies of scale which, while increasing production economies, causes havoc with the environment as greater concentrated output discharges greater concentrated waste material. The pressure of population leads to spatial aggrandizement
thus generating proportionate expansions in transportation in
preservation of the social and economic unity, resulting in
proportionate declines in open space and environmental conser-

[31] Stewart L. Udall, *The Quiet Crisis* (New York: Holt, Rinehart,
and Winston, 1963), pp. 160–161.

vation. Increases in population, albeit causing greater social interaction and cultural diversification, produce frictions, annoyances, and environmental deterioration, such as noise, pollution, and odors.

The spatial pattern of local public economies is a means of coping with accelerating expenditures for water, sewage disposal, and transportation. Large initial investments and heavy fixed costs, with decreases in unit costs of production with larger outputs, rationally call for economies of scale which can only be achieved through governmental cooperation.[32]

Despite the awareness of common problems and the network of interdependencies that can be resolved through concerted areawide planning, urban development has been impeded by the "political jungles with thickets of competing governments."[33] Like their governments, urban communities have persisted in competing, rather than cooperating with each other. Community amenities have produced debilitating spillover effects on neighboring communities; urban renewal has sought the amelioration of a community's economic competitive posture *vis a vis* its neighbors, with an indifference to the relocation of displaced residents within a regional context; and local public economies have often averted the need to provide needed public services, to the detriment of surrounding communities.

For example, air pollution is a boundary-transcending phenomenon which is not amenable to localized control.

> The private cost to the individual or the local government is most often cheaper if he does pollute than if he has to use expensive disposal equipment. If the water is polluted, it is the people downstream who are affected. If the air is polluted, it is the people in the direction of the wind. This is an instance where the private costs of pollution are almost always less than the costs to the rest of society. Pollution is a way of relinquishing what should be your responsibility to someone else who is usually anonymous.

[32] Thompson in Eldredge (ed.), Vol. I, *op. cit.*
[33] Chinitz in Chinitz (ed.), *op. cit.*, p. 107.

Thus pollution is one of those rare situations where social costs exceed private costs.[34]

The indifference of individuals and local governments to the effects of singular acts is creating intolerable social costs with far-reaching consequences. The post-industrial world as typified by the urban mass is beginning to seriously threaten the ecological balance thereby posing a danger to man. The modern urban conglomeration is a product of modern technology and consumption resulting from a post-war population growth and its concentration in specific areas. This excess of human numbers in a fragmented and parochial governmental system is in an inchoate process of formulating a rational concern with its growth and development while handicapped by a political system which abjures the subordination of localism to wider considerations.

The leveling off of the growth of urbanism has not curtailed the growth of urban areas. Despite an incipient respite from urbanization, urban areas have continued to grow, spatial development has continued to spread, and by-product problems have continued to mount.

Clearly modern urbanization is best understood in terms of its connection with economic growth, and its implications are best perceived in its latest manifestations in advanced countries. What becomes apparent as one examines the trend in these countries is that urbanization is a finite process, a cycle through which nations go in their transition from agrarian to industrial society. The intensive urbanization of most of the advanced countries began within the past one hundred years; in the underdeveloped countries it got underway more recently. In some of the advanced countries its end is now in sight. The fact that it will end, however, does not mean that either economic development or the growth of cities will necessarily end.[35]

[34] Marshall I. Goldman, "Pollution: The Mess Around Us," *Controlling Pollution, the Economics of a Cleaner America,* Marshall I. Goldman, (ed.) (Englewood Cliffs, N.J.: Prentice-Hall, Inc., 1967), pp. 10–11.

[35] Kingsley Davis, "The Urbanization of the Human Population," in *Cities, op. cit.,* p. 9.

The key to the growth of urban areas is population growth for, "as long as the human population expands, cities will expand too, regardless of whether urbanization increases or declines."[36] According to an Urban Land Institute Projection, by the year 2000 city dwellers will constitute 90 percent of the population of the United States, and 60 percent of them will inhabit 7 percent of the land, concentrating in three large metropolitan areas. Each of these large metropolitan areas will be known as megalopolis,[37] and will be located in three geographic areas:

> One megalopolis reaching from west of Chicago to Maine and down the Atlantic coast to south of Norfolk, a second stretching down California from 150 miles north of San Francisco to the Mexican border, and a third extending the length of the Florida peninsula.[38]

Today, 70 percent of California's population is concentrated in the Los Angeles and San Francisco metropolitan areas. Of the remainder, 12 percent is clustered in the Sacramento, San Diego and San Joaquin metropolitan areas, with a scant 18 percent distributed elsewhere. Thus, in heavily developed California, two-thirds of the population lives on one percent of the land.[39] Both the present distribution of population and predicted growth pattern presage the amorphous megalopolis of tomorrow.

Constantin A. Doxiadis, the Greek planner who founded Ekistics, "the science of human settlements," predicts the population explosion will last between 100 and 150 years. He

---

[36] *Ibid.*, p. 22.

[37] *Webster's New World Dictionary of the American Language,* 1968 edition, describes megalopolis as "an extensive, heavily populated, continuously urban area, including any number of cities."

[38] The President's Council on Recreation and Natural Beauty, *From Sea to Shining Sea—A Report on the American Environment, Our Natural Heritage,* (Washington, D.C.: U.S. Government Printing Office, 1968), p 89.

[39] John T. Middleton, "Science and Environmental Control, Smog-Free Air and Its Price," *Proceedings of Symposium on California and Challenge of Growth* (San Diego: University of California, San Diego, June, 1963).

believes that it will not be until toward the middle of the twenty-first century or, at the latest, by the beginning of the twenty-second,

> . . . when projected population curves for the entire world are expected to show a considerable slowing down, a point of physical saturation is expected to be reached; this is seen as a sort of saturation of the physical space available on the earth which can be economically inhabited, following the attainment of the highest practically obtainable densities within these areas.[40]

Doxiadis envisions the spreading of the megalopolis "into a kind of unified system of urbanized areas spanning the globe,"[41] which he calls the "ecumenopolis," meaning "the city spanning the entire habitable portion of the earth."[42] He predicts the population of ecumenopolis will reach from a low of twenty billion to a high of fifty billion human beings! The population estimate is expected to be realized by the year 2030 AD at the earliest, 2075 AD as the median, and 2120 AD at the latest! Technology is expected to increase commensurably with population but the scarcity of water and energy are expected to become serious limitations. Despite these dire forebodings, Doxiadis fatalistically cautions that over the "next century we are limited to shaping and directing population and urban growth but must not attempt to interfere with or blunt that growth."[43]

Without the problems of megalopolis, let alone ecumenopolis, our myriad present urban problems are approaching crisis proportions. Urban population concentrations—in the metropolitan, or regional age—is the cause of "garbage" in the en-

---

[40] "The Ecumenopolis Concept," *Ekistics, Reviews on the Problems and Science of Human Settlements,* Vol. 20, No. 116, July, 1965, p. 15.

[41] *Ibid.,* p. 18.

[42] *Ibid.*

[43] George Macinko, "Land Use and Urban Development," *The Subversive Science, Essays Toward an Ecology of Man,* Paul Shepard and Daniel McKinley, (eds.) (Boston: Houghton Mifflin Co., 1969), p. 371.

vironment, overcrowded highways, growing slums, deteriorating school systems, rising crime rates, riots, and so on. The effects of the environmental deterioration are reflected in the weather, the supply of oxygen, plant and animal ecological balance, and mental health.

> Too many cars, too many factories, too much detergent, too much pesticide, multiplying contrails, inadequate sewage treatment plants, too little water, too much carbon dioxide—all can be traced easily to too many people.[44]

Ecosystem and Man

Population growth has influenced urban development, industrial growth, energy production, present transportation systems, and each has had a detrimental effect upon the quality of the environment.[45] A report by the Surgeon General's Committee on Environmental Health Problems, published in 1962, stated:

> Increasing populations and increasing concentrations of people into urban areas of the United States have accentuated environmental problems in two important, related ways: (1) as our air, water, and land resources are fixed, increasing populations decrease the quantity of each of these basic necessities available to the individual; (2) with increasing amounts of waste products concentrated in areas with growing populations, the relative effects of these wastes on man are increasing at an ever-expanding rate. These threats are of an insidious nature, a form of creeping paralysis which, if not recognized and corrected, can lead to urban stagnation and death as surely as the most violent epidemic.[46]

Air pollution, the atmospheric result of a complex of industrial solid, liquid, and gaseous refuse from a multitude of

[44] Dr. Paul R. Ehrlich, *The Population Bomb* (New York: Ballantine Books, 1969), pp. 66–67.

[45] Middleton, *op. cit.*

[46] Lewis Herber, *Crisis in Our Cities* (Englewood Cliffs, N.J.: Prentice-Hall, Inc., 1965), p. 21.

sources is particularly noxious and deleterious to high-density compact areas. Air pollution is further exacerbated by atmospheric conditions and climatic and geographic factors, and has gone beyond the stage of being a nuisance to one that is now a serious health hazard.

The Meuse Valley of Belgium suffered the first recorded disaster in 1930 when 60 fatalities and 6,000 illnesses occurred because of a serious condition of air pollution. Donora, Pennsylvania, in 1948, reported 20 deaths and 43 percent of its population, incapacitated by air pollution. During London's air pollution disaster of 1952 4,000 fatalities were recorded.

Air pollution is broken down into the "London type" and the "Los Angeles type."[47]

> Smoke, soot, and sulphur compounds [sulphur dioxide, trioxide, and sulphuric acid] form the main ingredients of what is commonly called, "London-type air pollution," the traditional form of air pollution that prevails in the older cities of the United States, such as New York and Philadelphia.[48]

The "Los Angeles" type, a product of the overabundance of automobiles, is caused by petroleum wastes, sunlight, and the meteorological conditions of bad ventilation and temperature inversions, in an overindustrialized area. It is the

> . . . incomplete combustion in the automobile engine and losses caused by venting of the crankcase and evaporation of gasoline from carburator and tank that result in the emission of unburned gasoline and its partially oxodized irritating products, as well as large quantities of carbon monoxide, oxides of nitrogen and hydrocarbons.[49]

Both the "London" and the "Los Angeles" varieties cause irritation of exposed living membranes—the eyes, throat, and respiratory passageways—and result in asthma, pneumonia,

[47] *Ibid.*
[48] *Ibid.*, p. 43.
[49] Report of the Environmental Pollution Panel, President's Science Advisory Committee, "Restoring the Quality of Our Environment," (The White House, November, 1965), p. 63

emphysema, bronchitis, and heart attack.[50] Property damage from air pollution affects clothing, home furnishings, buildings, machinery, roads and public installations, and has totalled billions of dollars.[51]

Water pollution is another example of population growth and industrialization exploiting a vital natural resource, as cities, farms, and industries dump wastes into rivers and streams "in many cases without plan, without controls, and without even any particular thought."[52] Water is being polluted by sewage and industrial solids, radioactive wastes, and agricultural and industrial chemical excrement.[53] Polluted waterways are traditional carriers of bacterial diseases—such as cholera and typhoid fever—but modern science and conventional water-purification methods have effectively neutralized these dread bacteria. Contemporary industrial and human excrement in the waterways, however, are sorely testing available resources for health and sanitation maintenance,[54] as polluted water may soon become the breeding ground for the uncontrollable and "most sinister pathogen" of all—the virus, whose watery route has been provided by man "from flush toilet to the kitchen tap."[55] Water pollution, virus or no, has managed to kill off fish, and higher forms of vegetation, deprive man of potable water, and generally turn waterways into sewers, "evil appearing, odious and virtually devoid of life."[56]

Man has throughout history struggled to control nature. Man's knowledge has developed a technology that has altered his style of living and his environment. His knowledge has

[50] The recorded air pollution tragedies were attributed to "London" type pollution, however. Herber, *op. cit.*

[51] *Ibid.*

[52] *Ibid.*

[53] *Ibid.*

[54] Most water-treatment plants are ill equipped to cope with radioactive wastes, detergents, insecticides, herbicides, plastics, abrasives, food and fuel additives, pharmaceuticals, and petroleum derivatives which could cause unforetold short and long-run health and genetic problems. *Ibid.*

[55] *Ibid.*

[56] *Ibid.*

provided him with an enormous amount of goods and services and afforded him heretofore unknown leisure and amenities, all the more to improve his living condition and the enjoyment of his environment. Vast energy borrowed from nature developed an industrial system that brought men to live together, to share in experiences, abilities, cultures, and talent, for the broadening of man's outlook and the excitement of the diversity of urban life.

Technology's attempt at a beneficent control of nature has been obviated by deleterious side effects that now threaten to destroy it. The wastes generated by industrial processes have "poured into the water, released into the air, buried in the soil, or scattered about the landscape."[57] Thus, as man reached the threshold of technocratic mastery over nature, and the arrival of the age of enlightened plenty, nature, in its agony, has spewed back the residue of man's civilization, involving man in it, as if to warn that man is but an actor, among other actors, in nature's ecological system and the "good life" can never be, if at odds with the ecosystem.

> The modern technology which has added much to our lives can also have a darker side. Its uncontrolled waste products are menacing the world we live in, our enjoyment, and our health. The air we breathe, our water, our soil and wildlife, are being blighted by the poisons and chemicals which are the byproducts of technology and industry.[58]

Ecology, the natural "web-of-life," relates all organisms in a complex network of interdependencies, with the action of one causing a series of chain reactions to ultimately affect all.

> The pond is an example. Its ecology includes all events: the conversion of sunlight to food and the foodchains within and around it, man drinking, bathing, fishing, plowing the slopes of the watershed, drawing a picture of it, and formulating theories about the world based on

---

[57] *From Sea to Shining Sea, op. cit.,* pp. 17–19.
[58] Lyndon Baines Johnson, "Beauty for America," in Eldredge (ed.), Vol. I, *op. cit.,* p. 239.

what he sees in the pond. He and all the other organisms at and in the pond act upon one another, engage the earth and atmosphere, and are linked to other ponds by a network of connections like the threads of protoplasm connecting cells in living tissues.[59]

The challenge to man and his burgeoning numbers, in the ecosystem, is to realize his interdependence with his environment and not become "an all sterilizing force" threatening all other life forms in his selfish drive for self-aggrandizement.[60] The faculty of intelligence affords man the opportunity for choice of type of ecological behavior, but this historic potential for rational organic evolution is obviated by the irresistible drive toward technology and the inability to curtail harmful population growth.

> In a cumulative chain of causation there is necessarily integration between many factors; this together with the fact that the final outcome of a cumulative social process always depends upon the concurrence of circumstances makes it possible to shift part of the causal "responsibility" to one or the other factors. While this will always be possible and while it may serve a purpose in a debate, it defeats the search for truth. The truth of the matter is that it is the whole cumulative process of unrestrained concentration of industries and the subsequent growth of urban communities which gives rise to the contamination of the environment beyond the levels of concentration of pollutants that might be said to be compatible with human health. It is this process of unrestrained concentration, regardless of climate and topography, which gives rise to the social costs.[61]

The post-industrial age must accommodate the requisites of its advanced civilization that demands unparalleled amenities and comforts and the largesse of consumption requiring all of the abilities of modern technology to fulfill, while adhering to

[59] Paul Shepard, "Introduction: Ecology and Man, A Viewpoint," in Shepard and McKinley (eds.), *op. cit.,* p. 4.

[60] Macinko, *op. cit.*

[61] Karl William Kapp, "Social Costs of Business Enterprise," in Goldman (ed.), *op. cit.,* p. 85.

ecological sanity. In the process of trying to reconcile the dilemma, Lewis Mumford's description of an urban population,

> . . . as people who do without pure air, who do without sound sleep, who do without a cheerful garden or playing space, who do without the very sight of the sky and the sunlight, who do without free motion, spontaneous play, or a robust sexual life,[62]

is dangerously approaching reality.

The existence of urban economic, social, and environmental interdependencies reveals the presence of a complexity of urban systems. The communality of urban forms and functions and the affecting interrelationships of one sector's patterns and pressures upon all interconnected sectors underscores the validity of input-output studies of generalities and specifics of interregional flows of activities and investigations of social organizations and mobility.[63] Regional income and population distribution, industrial mix and placement, transportation network, and public and private acts upon the environment, are influential upon all participating actors in the urban system.

> Ecology "the study of the relation of an organism to its total environment" has a counterpart in the field of technology with the development of systems analysis. A space missile, for example, is a combination of systems— each composed of subsystems—for propulsion, guidance, enclosure of passengers, and communications. The effects of all activities within each system and subsystem must be measured not only by the efficiency of the single system but also by their effects on other systems.

> Similarly, a human environment is composed of various systems and subsystems, including a residential system, an industrial system, an agricultural system, a communications system, and a transportation system. The goal of all these systems should be a total environment capable of satisfying the broadest range of human needs. The effects

---

[62] Herber, *op. cit.*, p. 121.

[63] Melvin M. Webber, "The Roles of Intelligence Systems in Urban-Systems Planning," in Eldredge (ed.), Vol. II, *op. cit.*

of activities within each of these systems must be evaluated for their influence on all other systems constituting the environment. A transportation system, for example, should be measured not merely for its efficiency in moving people and goods, but for its effect on residential neighborhoods, parks, schools, the distribution of commercial and industrial facilities, the total development of the community and of the individuals who compose it.[64]

[64] *From Sea to Shining Sea, op. cit.,* pp. 23–25.

III

Government Reform
In the Metropolis

Governmental Pattern in the Metropolis

FRAGMENTATION IS the key feature of the American political-governmental system. According to the Committee for Economic Development, in 1967, there were 20,703 local government units serving metropolitan areas, which is one-fourth of the local government total in the nation. The average was 91 local governments for each metropolitan area, and 46 per metropolitan county.

Most metropolital residents are served by at least four separate local governments—a county, a municipality or a township, a school district, and one or more special districts whose functions range from garbage collection to mosquito control.[1]

The structure of government in metropolitan areas is oblivious to the existence of physical, social and economic interdependencies. Instead, it is a "jungle of competing, overlapping,

[1] *Reshaping Government in Metropolitan Areas* (New York: Committee for Economic Development, 1970), p. 13.

uncoordinated independent political units."[2] Added to the scene of political existentialism is the recognition that political boundaries are no longer descriptive of physical patterns of settlement nor, of course, of activity patterns among settlements. Despite the increasing complexities of urban communities and their diverse interactions, the prevalent conception of the urban phenomenon remains the physically delineated, discrete nodal settlements governable as distinct municipalities. This adherence to the principle of place-defined territorialities is thus suited to the existing areally and functionally bounded authorities.

Inhibitions to Change. Opposition to an institutional framework suitable for articulating the common needs of interdependent communities is rooted in philosophic, legal, and political principles. The philosophic framework is vested in the liberal individualism of the Utilitarians, whose credo was that "the individual knows his own interest best," and that "the free pursuit of individual egoisms maximizes welfare."[3] The penchant for localism—"home rule"—is a consanguineous transliteration of the nineteenth century "laissez-faire," and was applied to maximize local autonomy and to provide a "market choice" of community services.[4] "Home rule" has also been revered for its approximation of the majoritarian democratic ideal. A form of government "close to the people" is a government seen as most responsive to local needs insulated from outside interference.

The legal framework has worked to legitimize the social-philosophical framework of home-rule by legislative enact-

---

[2] Advisory Commission on Intergovernmental Relations, *Urban America and the Federal System, Commission Findings and Proposals,* M-47, (Washington, D.C.: October, 1969), p. 74.

[3] Derek Senior (ed.), *The Regional City, An Anglo-American Discussion of Metropolitan Planning* (Chicago: Aldine Publishing Co., 1966), p. 38.

[4] U.S Congress and Senate, Subcommittee on Intergovernmental Relations of the Committee on Government Operations, in Cooperation with the Joint Center for Urban Studies of the Massachusetts Institute of Technology and Harvard University. *The Effectiveness of Metropolitan Planning* (Washington, D.C.: June 30, 1964).

ments. Local government is established in state constitutions, statutes, and legislative codes.

The legislative framework governing the operation of local units of government has served to encourage greater fragmentation of government at the expense of comprehensive structural integration.[5]

This is reflected in legislation stipulating that the formation or dissolution of a municipal corporation is the prerogative of its residents. Conversely, the integration of several communities is dependent upon "concurrent majorities" which is to say, each community exercises an absolute veto over the prospective consolidation.

Political values also inhibit the development of areawide institutions. Basic to this is the financial discordance over the allocation of encumbrances for common projects. The discrepancy in metropolitan fiscal resources impedes the institutionalization of solidarity between the wealthier and the poorer communities. Along with the existing socio-economic disharmonies, there exists a fundamental city-suburban schism that creates added difficulties for the reconciliation of interests on behalf of areawide considerations.

Indeed, a rise of the status differential city-to-suburb, and the symbolizing of that differential in terms of race, would make metropolitan community even more elusive than it is now. We must reckon with the fact that already in the state legislatures, it is city-suburb voting blocs which have replaced the urban-rural deadlock.[6]

Social and racial antipathy has been an obstacle to metropolitan community with Negroes reluctant to join an areawide

[5] Winston W. Crouch and Beatrice Dinerman, *Southern California Metropolis, A Study in Development of Government for a Metropolitan Area* (Berkeley, Calif.: University of California Press, 1963), p. 366.

[6] Henry C. Hart, "The Dawn of a Community-Defining Federalism," "Intergovernmental Relations in the United States," *The Annals of the American Academy of Political and Social Science* (Philadelphia: May, 1965), pp. 152–153.

entity for fear of losing their newly gained political leverage in the central city, and suburban whites abominating the incursion and added financial burden of city-dwelling minorities. Local established interests and the apathy of the general public have also contributed to the perpetuation of governmental polycentricism.[7]

Rationale for governmental integration. Laissez-faire in the political system has become dysfunctional to goal-seeking, by favoring only those localities which profit from it, and by encouraging internecine warfare among the communities competing for sustaining resources. The sanctity of home rule has begun to conflict seriously with the requirements of modern service standards that can only be met by public performance on a metropolitan scale. Home rule has tended to signify poor public performance because of its diffusion of authority in an interdependent urban community which transcends defined political boundaries. However, the cultural entrenchment of localism, insofar as its applicability to majoritarian democratic principles, has induced even the most avid champions of metropolitan community to propound an affinity for its values. Their task is not to erase home rule but to temper it to contemporary urban realities.[8] This was, essentially, the theme of Hugh Pomeroy's address before the National Conference on Metropolitan Problems, at East Lansing, Michigan, on April 29, 1956:

> Local governmental autonomy can have justification—and ultimately, validity—only as it is accompanied by responsibility, a realization by the individual municipality, government and people, of being an integral part of an intercommunity composite, with an acceptance of obligations based on that relationship. And the primary obligation is that of acceptance of some limitation of freedom of action in the interest of the greater good.[9]

[7] Advisory Commission on Intergovernmental Relations, *Factors Affecting Voter Reactions to Governmental Reorganization in Metropolitan Areas,* Summary of Report M-15, September, 1965.

[8] Crouch and Dinerman, *op. cit.*

[9] U.S., Congress, House, A Study Submitted to the Intergovernmental Relations Subcommittee of the Committee on Government

The premise of governmental reform is the need for an institutional framework to attend to the metropolitan area as a coherent whole.[10] This entails a form of authority permitting the solution of interrelated problems, albeit in a form which differentiates between areawide requirements and those bearing a smaller orientation. Consistently, it would suggest a modification of governmental structures to allow for areawide foci simultaneously with the retention of local integrity in the management of small-scale and noninterdependent affairs. The engagement with governmental reform, however, is largely articulated in terms of spatial place-areas. Disenchanted with the performance of authorities confined to small place-bounded areas, interest has concentrated upon the realization of action bodies responsive to a systematic treatment of larger settlement place perplexities. Thus, jurisdictional distinctions are characterized according to problems peculiar to neighborhood place communities—refuse collection, local streets, small parks, and the like—and problems of common interest to the larger place-communities, which among various functional tasks also invariably call for metropolitan spatial planning.[11]

The regard for the distention of place-communities has been forced by the activity patterns throughout metropolitan areas. Initially, the rapidly growing central cities agitated for extraterritorial functional domination over precious resources necessary for the operation of services demanded by their constituents. This resulted in bitter conflicts between the hardpressed cities and their environs, so that it took long and arduous negotiations and court battles until the cities were allowed to undertake such functions as water provision and waste disposal outside their territorial limits.

Operations by the Advisory Committe on Intergovernmental Relations, *Metropolitan America: Challenge to Federalism,* 89th Cong., 2d Sess., October, 1966.

[10] Webb S. Fiser, *Mastery of the Metropolis* (Englewood Cliffs, N.J.: Prentice-Hall, Inc., A Spectrum Book, 1962), p. 4.

[11] Melvin M. Webber, "The Urban Place and the Nonplace Urban Realm," in Webber, *et al., Explorations into Urban Structure* (Philadelphia: University of Pennsylvania Press, 1964)

The California situation became so disturbing that in 1963, Governor Brown, in consultation with the state-wide associations of local officials, induced the legislature to establish local government formation commissions in each county to bring order. Each commission, composed of two county officers, two city officers, and a public member, must approve all annexations, incorporations, or formation of special districts within its county in future.[12]

A consensus among municipalities, located within a place-region, for the necessity of attracting business and industry, and an awareness that the location of such enterprises posit favorable effects upon the whole region, has encouraged intra-regional cooperation. This has been necessitated by a community's competitive disadvantage of its marketing, resources, and transportation potential *vis a vis* those of a region. Hence, for a community-within-a-region to be able to induce a favorable industrial locational decision, it must persuade the commercial enterprise of the region's superior attractions. In this context it has been logical and expedient for political jurisdictions to venture cooperatively into the competitive arena for market allocations, rather than compete among neighbors and thereby lose out to a functionally cohesive region.

The growing expense of public services and facilities and the recognition of some of their spillover effects, have necessarily caused the utility of efficiency and economy to be determinants in governmental operations. The myriad local units within a larger place-region, albeit admirably suited to the simpler requirements of the seventeenth and eighteenth centuries, are no longer functionally capable of adjusting to the needs of contemporary complexities. A comprehension of this condition has encouraged jurisdictional evaluation of sundry practicabilities for area wide cooperation, and even joint service provision, for the attainment of efficient scales of operation.

The provision of urban services concerns itself with the boundaries of the institutions designed for optimum utility. The conceptualization of appropriate boundary relationships seeks

[12] Winston W. Crouch, "Conflicts and Cooperation Among Local Governments in the Metropolis," in *Annals, op. cit.,* p. 66.

to attain a balance between the efficiency of uniformity and scale and the prudence of small-scale responsiveness and flexibility. A suitable governmmental framework would provide for economy of scale and functional control while committing to adequate political representation and local self-determination.

Factor determinants for areawide mechanisms. There are a number of critical factors that offer guidelines for the designation of suitable regional devices. The National Service to Regional Councils lists them as: area of the problem; geographical area; efficiency and economy; coordination of effort; political feasibility; and citizen control.[13]

The "area of the problem" relates to the essential inclusion of all jurisdictions—city, suburban and fringe—joined by the mutuality of phenomena or problems, in the proposed areawide organization. The "geographic area" signifies all affected municipalities, and of sufficient dimension for solving boundary-transcending environmental problems. Conflict resolution and the establishment of regional priorities are essential prerequisites for an areawide "coordination of effort." Any realistic formulation of regional alternatives must regard "political feasibility" as the criterion for program implementation. Finally, since the *raison d'etre* of a newly-created regional process is to improve public services it should be responsive to the needs of the public.

> The device, then, must be consistent with the principle of citizen control, either through direct participation in the decision-making process or, perhaps more realistically, through having the decision makers responsible to the citizen through some system of selection, such as elections. In this manner, then, a system of solving areawide problems is constructed which includes a process of political accountability.[14]

The regional device is compelled to comply with the factors criteria in order to attain the extent of resources, commit-

[13] National Service to Regional Councils, *Regional Alternatives,* Special Report #2 (Washington, D.C.: May, 1968).

[14] *Ibid.,* p. 3.

ment, and coverage unobtainable by individual jurisdictions, for the resolution of areawide issues. An area-wide instrumentality is expressly designed to overcome the limitations inherent in fragmented decision making by providing the means for coordinated policy making and delivery.

Regional Alternatives

There have been experiments with regional structures classifiable into four categories. First, the techniques for unitary action by the annexation and consolidation of all units to form a single level general-purpose jurisdiction. Second, the processes of unification, such as federation or amalgamation, wherein local units retain dominion over internalized functions but cede responsibility for area-wide problems to a broader-based authority. Third, the limited-transfer-of-function device of local governments according specific tasks to another agency or governmental unit. Finally, there are the cooperative mechanisms of area-wide institutions, formed by and responsible to the member local governments, for the execution of one or more area-wide functions.[15]

Unitary Approach. This method is realized by the aggrandizement—"annexation"—of surrounding land by a community, or by the merger of two or more municipalities into a "consolidated" unit. The one general-purpose government approach affords efficiency and economy of scale in its unified and coordinated handling of area-wide functions. However, its centralized nature creates an aura of institutional anonymity associated with the expected losses to local autonomy, governmental accessibility, and regard for local idiosyncrasies.

Annexations and consolidations have been impeded by suburban-rural favoring legislation allowing a single unit's

---

[15] *Regional Alternatives,* op. cit.; John C. Bollens and Henry J. Schmandt, *The Metropolis, Its People, Politics, and Economic Life* (New York: Harper and Row Publishers, 1965); Anthony H. Anderson, "The Movement Towards Regional Government," unpublished Master's Thesis, Department of Government, Claremont Graduate School, Claremont, Calif., April, 1970.

rejection to void a proposed merger. To achieve "annexation" generally requires an approving popular majority in the unincorporated territory; "consolidation" laws commonly necessitate the obtaining of separate favorable majorities in each unit proposed for the areal unification. Under the circumstances, most annexations occurred prior to the enactments of legislation giving a controlling leverage to the residents of outlying areas, and these were mostly of contiguous unincorporated tracts.

> Since the highly fortuitous combination of these two circumstances—liberal or equitable annexation laws and sizable adjoining unincorporated land—has generally been necessary in the postwar [World War II] years to accomplish large annexations, such expansions have been mostly confined to certain types of metropolitan areas, particularly those of small or medium size, such as Oklahoma City, Phoenix, Mobile, San Antonio, Charlotte, and Amarillo.[16]

The major drawback to "annexation" is that the territorial limits of the urban-place region continually widen, thereby adding new autonomous municipalities and expanded activity patterns within the conceptualized physical definition. Thus, "regardless of the total amount of territory annexed by any city in recent years, the current boundaries of that city are far short of being the same as the territorial limits of the metropolis."[17]

Integration Processes. There are at least three forms within this classification: unified county government, geographical or functional consolidation, or federated government.

> These alternatives distinguish themselves in that there is in this class the elimination or amalgamation of governments or functions of governments, and the by-product of this structural change is one unit of government with area-wide responsibility. Although the existing units of government need not be eliminated to achieve this purpose, certain

---

[16] Bollens and Schmandt, *op. cit.,* p 415.
[17] *Ibid.,* p. 417.

of the functions and prerogatives of the local units accrue to the area-wide government.[18]

Unified County Government—The unified county is a county which is the recipient of one or more local governmental functions and services. Ordinarily, the county appropriates the functions bearing a regional impact, while the local authorities reserve control over limited-scale issues. The ultimate of a unified county government is that it can become a true metropolitan government by being the beneficiary of a simultaneous reallocation of all municipal functions through state constitutional revision or local charter provisions. If this existed in practice then unified county government, or rather, comprehensive metropolitan county, would be included in the preceding classification of "unitary approaches." However, in actuality, there are but two forms of the unified county. The first involves a limited form of functional shifts; the second, a piecemeal and evolutionary extension of services through city-county negotiations. In either case the local jurisdictions retain their integrity.

The obstacles to the realization of the unified urban county as a true metropolitan government are legal, structural, functional, and financial. Legally, the provision for this concept is nonexistent in many states, and state constitutional revisions would be required for its authorization. The second hindrance is the structural unpreparedness of many county governments for the assumption of enlarged urban tasks and services. Counties were created to operate as geographic subdivisions of the state government performing as local surrogates for certain administrative obligations and providing services to rural residents. The transition to comprehensive urban functions would entail restructuring the counties' administrative framework and the method of constituting the governing body. County government must develop a structural integration capable of efficient functional performance, and a process of political responsibility and responsiveness to the needs of an urban constituency. Finally, the counties must overcome their

[18] *Regional Alternatives, op. cit.,* p. 4.

financial strait-jacket. Unless constitutional tax limitations and undue reliance upon the property tax are altered, the counties will be financially impotent to address themselves to the functional requirements of an urban-county government.

The development of a unified county affords a coordinated multifunctional approach to problem-solving on a manageable geographical scale. On the other hand, a unified county technique is only appropriate where area-wide problems are contained within the boundaries of a single county. Additionally, local interest representation is diluted in the process of conflict resolution and the setting of priorities, and the feasibility of the regional device is dependent upon the functional capability of the county government.

A noteworthy model of the unified county, metropolitan approach is Dade County, Florida, which includes the City of Miami. A county charter, adopted by a referendum in 1957, provided for a structurally integrated county government while retaining the existing twenty-six, later to become twenty-seven, municipalities. The county government was empowered with responsibilities over area-wide functions such as the construction of expressways, police and fire, mass transit systems and transportation, water and sewer, and the preparation and enforcement of comprehensive development plans. It was also authorized to acquire any function performed by a municipality that did not comply with minimal standards set by the county. The governing body of Metro Miami is a commission of 9 members; eight members are elected county-wide with residence requirements and the other is elected as mayor and serves as permanent board chairman.[19] The major accomplishments of the county government have been its streamlining and integrating of administrative functions. Its efficacy, however, is impaired by fiscal inadequacy and grudging support from the municipalities.[20]

A California modification of the unified county concept

[19] Based on the 1963 Amended Charter. The original charter called for representation by five members elected at large, five members elected by districts, and one official from each city exceeding 100,000 in population.

[20] Bollens and Schmandt, *op. cit.*

is the so-called "Lakewood Plan," a process wherein the municipalities contract the county for the provision of multi-functional services to the inhabitants of the contracted communities. The contract spells out the service levels and charges, but in no way affects the autonomy of the municipalities nor their ultimate responsibility for the services. This technique is an example of the city-county negotiations for piecemeal and evolutionary transfer of services to the larger place-region authority, to obtain the efficiency of economy of scale and uniformity.

Functional and Geographical Consolidation—is a method that refers to the coalescing of two or more jurisdictions into one unit of government which then affects the original units' powers and responsibilities. In reality, consolidation has adhered to county boundaries, and the process usually involves the county government's absorption of one or more municipalities within the county. The most conclusive form of city-county consolidation is the total merger of all local jurisdictions and the county government into a single authority, thereby making it a metropolitan government in form. Mutations of the ideal, practiced in the United States, might effect a city-county consolidation but retain the county as a unit for certain purposes, or, exempt some municipalities from the consolidation. The attainment of consolidation is generally contingent upon the approval of the voters in the affected jurisdictions, and state enabling legislation or constitutional amendment.

"With relatively few exceptions, reorganization proposals have been rejected by voters who apparently have been influenced more by arguments promising to keep the tax rate low and the government close to the people and free of corruption than by arguments stressing the correction of service inadequacies and the economical and efficient provision of services."[21]

Because of the difficulties—legal, cultural, and structural —for achieving governmental integration, the realization of

[21] Joseph F. Zimmerman, "Metropolitan Reform in the U.S.: An Overview," *Public Administration Review,* September/October, 1970, p. 531.

city-county consolidation has been sporadic, and invariably, in forms less than ideal. Four of the five consolidations, prior to 1910, occurred in the 1800's; and there have been five more consolidations, outside of Virginia since 1910.[22] Baton Rouge–East Baton Rouge Parish (1947), Nashville–Davidson County (1962), Jacksonville–Duval County (1968), Carson City and Ormsby County, Nevada (1969), and Indianapolis–Marion County (1970). The Nashville and Jacksonville consolidations kept their county governments as separate entities for a few functions; the Nevada consolidation was minor; the Indianapolis–Marion County merger excluded some municipalities within its jurisdiction; and, Baton Rouge–East Baton Rouge Parish retained a county (parish) government entity and did not include two small municipalities.[23] These five consolidations were exceptional in that common dissatisfactions with "duplication of services, overlapping jurisdictions, worsening area-wide problems, fragmentation of powers and responsibilities and alienation of the citizens from their governments"[24] overcame traditional persuasions against governmental reordering.

That three out of the last five consolidations had occurred in southern metropolitan areas which, generally, do not have highly competitive political systems, accounts for the argument that consolidation is easier obtained in an atmosphere lacking political competitiveness. This consideration was stated in 1957 by Edward C. Banfield, ". . . it will be difficult or impossible to integrate local governments where the two-party system operates . . . In effect, advocates of consolidation

---

[22] In Virginia, the state legislature "provided for judicial determination of proposals calling for the annexation of unincorporated territory or the consolidation of a city (or a town) and another town." The Virginia model, thus, affords a different route to jurisdictional integration by the vesting of power in an impartial body with the authority to impose boundary adjustments. Consequently, there has been an unusual proliferation of governmental reorganization in Virginia. Bollens and Schmandt, *op. cit.,* pp. 422–423.

[23] Ibid.; Anthony H. Anderson, *op. cit.;* Joseph F. Zimmerman, "Metropolitan Reform in the U.S.: An Overview," *op. cit.*

[24] "City-County Consolidation: Trend for the 1970's?" *Nation's Cities,* November, 1969, p. 28.

schemes are asking the Democrats to give up their control of the central cities or, at least, to place it in jeopardy."[25]

Federated Government—This mechanism involves the transfer of designated functions and power to a new level of government. This is a "two-tier" prototype in that the top tier—the federation—is charged with the responsibility for area-wide issues; the lower tier is made up of the federation's constituents—the local municipalities—which retain jurisdiction over functions and powers not delegated to the top tier.

Federated government has never been adopted in the United States because of the difficulties associated with its creation. The normal requirements for its establishment involve,

> . . . referenda in each participating jurisdiction, possibly state constitutional amendments, and acceptance of detailed procedures for differentiating functions and activities of local and regional governments by the local officials.[26]

An example of a federated technique is Metro Toronto, a government for the Toronto, Canada, metropolitan area. The criticality of certain service and financial problems gave the impetus for its development. However, the implantation of the federated idea resulted from a combination of uniquely Canadian political processes and traits: Metro Toronto's imposition by the Ontario provincial legislature upon recommendation of an impartial province-appointed quasi-judicial administrative agency; and, the Canadian lack of reverence for the sanctity of home rule, and culture of political deference.[27] These characteristics are in stark contrast to the highly competitive, non-deferential, and home-rule adherent local government systems endemic in the United States.

The federated approach provides for a clear delineation of the area-wide and local functions, facilitating the

[25] Edward C. Banfield, "The Politics of Metropolitan Area Organization," *Midwest Journal of Political Science,* May, 1957, p. 86
[26] *Regional Alternatives, op. cit.,* p. 5.
[27] Harold Kaplan, *Urban Political Systems, a Functional Analysis of Metro Toronto* (New York: Columbia University Press, 1967).

establishment of the optimal level of service. The structure and existence of local government is not threatened. The local governments are represented on the regional government providing needed coordination of effort. However, despite local control through representation on the federated government, the transfer of function weakens the local general purpose governments.[28]

Transfer of Responsibility. Unlike the "Unitary Approaches" and the "Integration Processes" which involve some intrinsic transformations in the dominion, structure and functions of existing units, "Transfer of Responsibility" does not affect any fundamental structural changes. It does, however, relegate one or more functional responsibilities and power to other agencies or units of government. These transfers, extrinsic to the *raison d'etre* of the existing units, occur on the assumption that the execution of the tasks would be improved by their relocation. Thus, functional responsibility is shifted in order to capitalize on economy and efficiency of scale and resources.

Transfer to the State—The states have had occasion to assume local functions when the localities had demonstrably been ineffective and inadequate in the treatment of their problems. These transfers become especially urgent when a municipality's functional performance in a specific area, as a matter of state policy, fails to achieve a state-wide minimum standard, or, when the consequences of the nonperformance spill over beyond the immediate area. As a result of these local inabilities, or in order to acquire efficiencies of scale and uniformity, the states have been actively impressing such functions as air and water pollution control, water supply, highway planning and construction, and comprehensive planning. In addition, interstate compacts are obviously the sole responsibility of the states. The negative aspects of these state activities are the erosion of local government power and prestige, and the inadequate provisions for local-state coordination in the provision of services affecting the localities.

[28] *Regional Alternatives, loc. cit.*

Special Purpose District—The ease with which special purpose districts are created—generally by legislative act alone —has led to their multiplicity, adding to the diffusion and un-coordination of governmental authority. However, these dis-tricts—such as water and sewer districts, transport authorities, and park districts—have been expedient devices for the execu-tion of singular functions, which do not necessarily coincide with existing political boundaries.

> In fact, one of the advantages of this approach is the flexibility of the boundaries which permits application to any area of manageable proportions to achieve a regional program.[29]

Additionally, the special purpose districts are not financial burdens upon the municipal authorities, as they possess an in-dependent tax collection capability.

Multi-purpose District—This technique has all of the ad-vantages of the special purpose district—

> . . . adaptation of an area-wide approach to common problems, fixing the costs to the benefited area, the relative ease of establishment facilitating a rapid response to critical problems, and the flexibility of boundaries per-mitting application to the problem area, irrespective of political boundaries.[30]

—and, in addition, because it is multifunctional, the multi-purpose distict provides a regional basis for policy and effort coordination. Additionally, the multifunctional district is not a static device but one that can expand to include new program interests at the will of the public. Another transcendency over the single-function district is manifested by its being the central axis for a myriad of activities and policies, thus facilitating constituent control.

> One example of the multi-purpose district approach is the Municipality of Metropolitan Seattle created in 1958. The enabling legislation authorizes the local govern-

[29] *Ibid.*, p. 6.
[30] *Ibid.*

ments of the area to transfer any or all of the following functions to the Metropolitan Corporation: sewage disposal, water pollution control, transportation, comprehensive planning, water, parks and solid waste disposal. As initially established, the critical pollution problem at Lake Washington brought about the transfer of the sewage disposal and water pollution control function to the district.[31]

The flexibility and functional efficacy of the multi-purpose district has earned it the rancor of some officials and citizens of local communities. As a multifunctional institution it poses a competitive threat to existing general purpose governments. Consequently, the proliferation of these districts, and their growth of influence, have been met with growing resistance as exemplified by the added prerequisites, such as voter approval, for their creation or expansion.

Intergovernmental Agreements or Contracts—These are *ad hoc* procedures for meeting non-controversial, administrative and service functions, such as health services, ambulance service, assessments, and central emergency communications facilities. These intergovernmental processes may be formal or informal; may involve an agreement for the joint performance of such functions and services as airports and port facilities; or, may include, on a contract basis, the transfer of functions from one authority to another.

Interlocal concerts are easily formalized, requiring little administrative or voter approval; achieve a measure of economy and efficiency in utilizing a larger geographic scale for the provision of services; and, pose no competition to existing structures. On the other hand, this procedure perpetuates piecemeal action on the part of local governments; postpones a comprehensive approach to problem-areas; and, is only feasible in perfunctory, non-conflict situations.

Cooperative Approach. A growing awareness of the urban complexities has served to diminish the zeal for governmental structural reform. The history of failure to effect major reorganizations coupled with the perception that the perplexities

[31] *Ibid.*

of the metropolis transcend the problem of myriad governments, have created a "predominant trend . . . to accept the
present governmental pattern as given and to seek ways to
accommodate the problems of the day within its general framework."[32] This becomes especially crucial with the recognition
of the shifting of the foci of power to higher levels of government, so that many of the determining decisions affecting the
metropolis are made by distantly removed agencies:

> . . . in Congress and at the state capitol; in the
> Department of Housing and Urban Development, the
> Bureau of Public Roads, and Department of Health,
> Education and Welfare; in the state highway commission
> and other state administrative agencies; and in the board
> rooms of national corporations.[33]

Because of the expansion of the urban universe and the
lack of formal governmental integration, the evolving pattern
of organizational arrangements have resulted from cooperative
action of local authorities. These voluntary regional mechanisms—most notably, transportation planning agencies, area-
wide planning and development commissions, economic development districts, councils of governments, and conferences of
local elected officials—have been formed as functional apparatus
to engage the common problem areas.

The transportation planning agencies and regional planning and development commissions are multi-jurisdictional
creatures of state enabling legislation for the purpose of fulfilling an area-wide functional responsibility. Although they enjoy the advantages of economies of scale, flexible functional
boundaries, and coordination of activities, they are hampered
in their effectiveness because of a unifunctional restrictiveness
and an insularity from political actors.

Economic development districts and local development districts, generally nonprofit corporations, are multi-jurisdictional

---

[32] Henry J. Schmandt, "Changing Directions," *Government of
the Metropolis, Selected Readings,* Joseph F. Zimmerman (ed.) (New
York: Holt, Rinehart, and Winston, Inc., 1968), p. 343.
[33] *Ibid.,* p. 344.

agencies devised for a multifunctional approach to a specific problem area. These agencies enjoy healthy federal subsidies encouraging their efficiency in improving areal economic and natural resources. However, their endeavors are handicapped in program implementation because of lack of local jurisdictional inclusion in their structures.

A regional framework exists that possesses all of the attributes of the unifunctional cooperative agencies and yet manages to overcome their shortcomings. This cooperative institutional framework—the councils of government, or conference of elected officials—is a multifunctional agency comprised chiefly of the elected officials of local government members of the councils.

> The multifunctional outlook and the inclusion of the responsible local elected officials distinguish the council of governments approach as the frontrunner of all other cooperative endeavors.[34]

Councils of Government—These institutions—councils, conferences, associations, or committees, have an assortment of legal bases: specific enabling legislation, general joint exercise of power statutes, intergovernmental agreements, corporate charters, or voluntary extralegal arrangements. The origination of councils of government is generally derived through the effort of local officials, either on their own volition or in response to external stimuli, or through the initiative of existing agencies.[35] The common purpose of these groups is to provide a forum for intergovernmental cooperation, and for the study and determination of area-wide problem solutions. The prevailing concept is that of the council as an advisory body to the member governments which alone have the authority to implement the council's recommendations. The frequent assertion is that councils of government are analogous to a United Nations. They are authoritatively impotent, and

[34] *Regional Alternatives, op. cit.,* p. 8.
[35] Royce Hanson, *Metropolitan Councils of Government,* Advisory Commission on Intergovernmental Relations, An Information Report, August, 1966.

dependent upon each individual member's inclusion of council decisions within the local policy framework, for functional implementation.

The model council's structure consists of the full membership of participating local jurisdiction, an Executive Committee derived from the full membership, and a professional staff. The full membership, an unwieldy body, meets infrequently and serves as a ratifying agent of Executive Committee activities. The Executive Committee, divided along functional interests and assisted by a professional advisory staff, discharges the actual tasks of the council. Functional programs vary according to the members' interests and normally include planning, transportation, air and water pollution control, government operations and research, uniform codes and standards, parks and open-space acquisition, and public safety.[36]

The decisive impetus to the development of councils of government originated with Federal legislation and policies requiring the existence of institutional frameworks performing area-wide coordination of Federal programs and comprehensive regional planning. Additionally, councils are heavily dependent on Federal financial support, because of insufficient contributions by the member units. The result of these linkages has been a Federal influence upon the operations and functional interest of the councils.

The essential contribution of the councils of government, albeit more of a potential rather than an actual accomplishment, is its axial situation *vis à vis* the urban and national political structures. The regional council, as representative of the local jurisdictions within its area, can perform as the spokesman for these governments to the state and federal authorities. By the same token,

> . . . to the extent that the councils become conduits for Federal assistance to both cities and suburbs, and to the extent that they are placed athwart the review process for metropolitan programs, the greater the prospects for

[36] John K. Parker, "Cooperation in Metropolitan Areas through Councils of Government," in Zimmerman (ed.), *op. cit* , p. 326.

their stability, durability, and for full participation by the cities.[37]

Thus, the prolific councils of government—with over 300 of them in 1972—appears the regional device most adapted to the cultural pattern of the American political system. The question remains whether it can become the institutional framework serving as the conduit for functional linkages between the urban and political systems.

Government and the Metropolis

The institutional alternatives for regional coherence understand the region as a defined place-community. However, today's metropolis is not a static, definable area. The urban regions are expanding and merging with each other to form megalopolises; and this amorphous growth is obviating the rationale for fixed place-oriented metropolitan governments. Shifting megalopolitan boundaries, through growth, would soon make a regional entity with static limits obsolescent. On the other hand, should the government be allowed to keep up with the expanding place-region, it will grow to sizes rivaling existing state and national jurisdictions. Governmental reorganization suited to a conceptualization of the region as a place-entity is a temporary palliative.

Under these conditions, the alteration of fundamental governmental structures becomes unreasonable and unadaptive to urban realities. Conversely, a vital transformation is that of functional integration with activity focused on place-conditions accommodated to nonplace interactions, and keyed to the crucial distinctions of spatial structures and patterns in the urban system. Planning as an activity, may become irrelevant, if tied to the form processes and static dimensions of place-bound institutions with "a banal sense of space location [creating] the illusion of the coincidence of political space with economic and human space."[38]

[37] Hanson, *op. cit.,* p. 20.
[38] Francois Perroux, "Economic Space: Theory and Applications," Friedmann and Alonso (eds.), *op. cit.,* p. 22.

IV

The Federal System
and Urban America

Character of the Federal System

THE ESSENTIAL distinction of the American political system are the aspects of its governmental non-centralization and intergovernmental collaboration. This implies the constitutional endurance of shared powers between a general government and more particularized governments, and the practice of their functional interaction. Daniel Elazar stated that the character of American federalism was formed by a precedent of fundamental principles and mechanisms for intergovernmental relations. These principles are: national supremacy; extensive national legislative and appropriation powers; noncentralized government; and, maximum local control. The mechanisms: non-disciplined, noncentralized party system; routinized legislative "interference" in administration; regular intergovernmental consultation; and, a system of grants-in-aid from higher to lower levels of government. Accordingly,

If the general government was early cast in the role of stimulator and partial supporter of such major governmental functions as education, internal improvements, and public welfare, the states—either directly or through their local subdivisions—were simultaneously cast in the role of managers and administrators of these functions. Policy-making for these programs became a joint state-federal activity.[1]

National Supremacy. The supremacy of the national government was prescribed in the Constitution. Article VI of the Constitution established the whole as greater than the sum of its constituent parts. In an afterthought, the 10th Amendment reaffirmed the states' partnership in the federal system: "The powers not delegated to the United States by the Constitution, nor prohibited by it to the States, are reserved to the States, respectively or to the people."[2] However, Article III, in installing the Supreme Court as the judicial primate in the nation, ordained the national level with the discretion of prescribing the extent of the powers reserved to the states. Subsequently, John Marshall's court concretized the role of the Supreme Court as the absolute and final judge in intergovernmental disputes.

> In its interpretation of this relationship, the Marshall Court defined the Supremacy Clause as meaning that the states could not interfere with the functioning of the national government, and that federal action, be it statute, treaty, court decision, or authorized administrative act, must prevail over state action.[3]

The supremacy of the national government was more firmly imbedded by the three Reconstruction amendments, and the Sixteenth Amendment

---

[1] Daniel J. Elazar, "The Shaping of Intergovernmental Relations in the Twentieth Century," The Annals of the American Academy of Political and Social Science, *Intergovernmental Relations in the United States* (Philadelphia: May, 1965), pp. 11–12.

[2] Clinton Rossiter, *1787: The Grand Convention* (New York: The MacMillan Co., 1966), p. 403.

[3] Terry Sanford, *Storm Over the States* (New York: McGraw-Hill Book Company, 1967), p. 19.

> . . . gave to the national government in 1913 what was to become the most powerful advantage of all, the income tax. Money is the source of power in government, and has enabled the national government to enter and influence even those fields of responsibility reserved to the states by the Tenth Amendment.[4]

Additionally, the national government became the panacea for all national problems when the states proved inefficient during the Depression. This established a contemporary precedent for looking to Washington in case of need.

National events, technology, and the acceleration of history have established the national government in a firm political dominance. Technology and communications gave rise to a national network of railroads and high speed highways, necessitating a comprehensive control over them. The economy has been marked by unprecedented growth and development. The expansion in private power has had to be balanced by public authority; economic stability has required large scale, centralized guidance; and major elements of the economy are reliant upon Washington contracts as well as being subject to national government regulation. Finally, the crises of international events and common public policy expectations have compelled a national scale perspective and thus, centralized direction.

> [The] constitutional issue [has been] settled conclusively against the states. The national government can now go a long way under the interstate commerce clause and the general welfare clause; and by grants-in-aid it can buy whatever additional authority Congress believes desirable. The future of the states rests not on constitutional protection but on political and administrative decisions. Indeed it rests in substantial measure on what the states do themselves. The issues of the future in this area are consequently political and administrative in nature. . . .[5]

[4] *Ibid.,* p. 20.
[5] Leonard D. White, "Selection from the States and the Nation," *Cooperation and Conflict, Readings in American Federalism,* Daniel

Sharing of functions. Despite the imbalance in the federal system, the courts have deemed the inviolability of the states as intrinsic to the existing political structure. *Texas* v. *White* (1869) was explicit in this regard:

> Not only . . . can there be no loss of separate and independent autonomy to the states, through their union under the Constitution, but it may be not unreasonably said that the preservation of the States, and the maintenance of their governments, are as much within the design and care of the Constitution as the preservation of the Union and the maintenance of the National government. The Constitution, in all of its provisions, looks to an indestructible Union, composed of indestructible States.[6]

However, the role of the states does not fulfill the conventional wisdom of the states-rights model, which assigns to the federal framework a competition between levels of government for distinct functions. Instead of the erroneous symbolization of the American form of government by a "layer cake," a more accurate conceptualization is that of Morton Grodzins' "marble cake."[7] This implies a sharing of functions among the three levels of the federal system. Policy output is the sum of shared intergovernmental activity, without neat differentiations of discrete "federal," "state," or "local" responsibilities. Axiomatic to the functional execution of the American federal system is "that the national government would use its superior resources to initiate and support national programs, principally administered by the states and localities."[8]

Noncentralized government. The noncentralization of the federal system is a product of constitutional and political devices which have formed unique traits in democratic repre-

---

J. Elazar *et al.* (eds.) (Itasca, Ill.: F. E. Peacock Publishers, Inc., 1969), p. 46.

[6] Elazar *et al.* (eds.), *op. cit.,* p. 44.

[7] Morton Grodzins, *Goals for Americans* (Englewood Cliffs, N.J.: Prentice-Hall, Inc., 1960).

[8] Elazar *et al.* (eds.), *op. cit.,* p. viii.

sentation, political party behavior, and public policy formulation.[9] American politics is formed around units of territory and therefore, the capability to gain representation in the councils of government is decided by contests for political control of these political properties. The contests for public office are conducted principally by coalitions of state and local party organizations, opposed as "Democrats" or "Republicans" for purposes of semblance of a national organizational solidarity. The nomenclatures of these differing groups become meaningful during national campaigns when the coalitions unite to elect their respective party's nominee to the presidency, a coveted prize of power, prestige, and patronage. Otherwise, these state and local organizations are virtually autonomous and responsible not to their parties, but to their geographic constituencies. Party discipline is negligible as constituent interests, particularly the powerful interest groups within the constituencies, bear far more influence upon the behavior of elected officials than do the demands of a political party.

The loose articulation between the various components of the federal government, weaknesses in the linkage system between party and government, and lack of programmatic orientation to public policy are characteristics of the federal political process providing channels of access to the decision-making centers of government. Professor Morton Grodzins has described these political "fissures" exploitable by individuals, groups, and all branches of government itself, as the "multiple crack" attribute of American politics.[10]

The channels of access to the decision making centers of government, afforded by the decentralized structure and function of the American federal system, have caused the phenomenon of a continuum of private and public groups. The

[9] Elazar, "Federalism and Intergovernmental Relations," in Elazar *et al.* (eds.), *op. cit.*

[10] Totton J. Anderson, "Pressure Groups and Intergovernmental Relations," *Intergovernmental Relations in the United States, op. cit.*, p. 119.

cause of functional representation is pressed by active interest groups integrated within the governmental process, and the public-private client collaboration wields authority in policy decisions by contributing to policy coordination. This has served to develop an intragovernmental "gamesmanship" where each branch, to enhance its bargaining strength, enlists the alliance of an "outside constituency" derived from some segment of society, to add to its "internal constituency" within government.[11] The administrative agencies are uniquely suited to this "gamesmanship," since they are often created in response to pressure group influence, and develop close ties with their clients in addition to a vertical functional compatibility with their bureaucratic counterparts within the political system.

The activities of interest groups are common to every policy making jurisdictional level within the federal framework. Exploitable breaches are provided by the struggles between the branches of government and in the contentions between national, state, and local authorities. Consequently, there is a constant flow of interaction and influence throughout the federal political hierarchy. However, because of the national level's leverage of financial predominance there is a focality to the system's interest activity.

> Centripetal forces are impelling the federal system toward functional, political nationalization. Public policy is being shaped between the downward pressures of vast expenditures of federal funds and the upper thrust of legislative interventionism on behalf of local interest regarding the manner in which those funds should be expended. The predictable result is the involvement of public officials on all levels of the federal system in pressure group activity with the inevitable concomitant of gradual nationalization of public policy.[12]

Intergovernmental Collaboration

The processes of intergovernmental activity in the American federal system ideally energizes all echelons of the political

[11] *Ibid.*
[12] *Ibid.*, p. 122.

hierarchy. The national government provides the impetus for public policy through comprehensive legislation and fiscal subvention; the states allocate the funds and administer the programs; and the local jurisdictions, with their services and programs influenced by the higher levels, are functionally linked to the states and the national government.[13]

There are many mechanisms attentive to intergovernmental relations within the federal framework. At the national level there are the following: (1) Intergovernmental Relations Subcommittees of the Senate and the House Committees on Government Operations; (2) a Presidential consultant on intergovernmental relations, and a special assistant for intergovernmental relations in the Office of Management and Budget; (3) Urban Affairs Council to aid the President in the development of a national urban policy; and (4) the Advisory Commission on Intergovernmental Relations. In addition, there are key officials throughout the bureaucracy responsible for intergovernmental functional coordination.[14]

The states are actively engaged in intergovernmental activities. Groups of states, with Congressional approval, negotiate interstate compacts, and have formed such interstate arrangements as the Port of New York Authority, and several compacts for the control and use of rivers. The Council of State Governments, a formally designated information exchange for the states, serves as a secretariat of ten organizations of state officials in addition to recommending policy, and providing research and technical advice on specialized problems. Finally, multilateral exchanges under the auspices of such agencies as the Council of Governors and the

[13] U.S., Congress, House, A Study submitted to the Intergovernmental Relations Subcommittee of the Committee on Government Operations by the Advisory Committee on Intergovernmental Relations, *Metropolitan America: Challenge to Federalism* (Washington, D.C.: U.S. Government Printing Office, October, 1966).

[14] William G. Colman, "The Role of the Federal Government in the Design and Administration of Intergovernmental Programs," *Intergovernmental Relations in the United States, op. cit.;* Lloyd Rodwin, *Nations and Cities, A Comparison of Strategies for Urban Growth* (Boston: Houghton Mifflin Co., 1970).

Council of State Governments provide recurring opportunities for interstate cooperation and coordination.[15]

Within the states, the localities are beginning to engage in fruitful collaborative devices. The conferences of local officials, or councils of government, as well as intercity and county-city contracts and interjurisdictional planning machinery, are significant manifestations of a new spatial awareness. Local officials have joined in functional interest groups, such as state leagues of city, county, or school officials, to influence policy affecting their areas of interest.[16]

A promising example of intergovernmental cooperation is the Appalachian program, a Federal-state undertaking to regenerate an economically depressed area stretching from northern Alabama and Mississippi to southern New York State.

> At the instigation of the governors of these states and by Congressional Act, the federal government and thirteen states have entered into a joint venture "to assist the region in meeting its special problems, to promote its economic development and to establish a framework for joint federal and state efforts toward providing the basic facilities essential to its growth and attacking its common problems and meeting its common needs on a coordinated and concerted regional basis.[17]

Congress has authorized parallel programs in the northeastern states, the Upper Great Lakes (the northernmost regions of Wisconsin, Minnesota, and Michigan), the Coastal plains (North Carolina, South Carolina, and Georgia), "Ozarkia" (Missouri, Arkansas, and Oklahoma), and the "Four Corners" (Utah, Colorado, Arizona and New Mexico).

> These programs place the major burden on the states and the governors, in planning, in policy making, in decision-making, and in administering the multi-state

[15] Sanford, *op. cit.;* Winston W. Crouch, "Conflict and Cooperation among Local Governments in the Metropolis," *Intergovernmental Relations in the United States, op. cit.*

[16] Crouch, *op. cit.*

[17] Sanford, *op. cit., p.* 115.

programs. Each state approaches the program differently and at different levels of sophistication—but this is a strength, not a weakness. It builds diversity where it is needed and modifies a monolithic approach to varied problems.[18]

Goal-seeking Outputs of the Federal Government .

Grants-in-aid. The federal government has many devices for influencing metropolitan regional activity. A major device is the grant-in-aid, a financial subvention to the echelons of the federal hierarchy for specific objectives. This assistance is conditioned on the recipients' subjection to federal administrative oversight and program guidelines. The program has grown from the first grant-in-aid in 1785 for local schools, to some 162 major aid programs in 1966, and a 1971 "Catalog of Federal Domestic Assistance" listing of 1,069 assistance programs administered by 62 different Federal departments, independent agencies, commissions, and councils.

The purpose of the grants is to enable state and local governments to deal with a broad variety of social and economic problems. The proportion of Federal financing to program-cost varies, with total or near-total subvention in some cases, and minimal aid in others. Federal grants-in-aid to the states and localities for all programs reached $30 billion in 1971; in fiscal year 1971 total grants expenditures were approximately at fourteen per cent of the federal budget, and fifteen percent of total state and local income.[19] The areas that have received significant financial support include: (1) transportation facilities; (2) redevelopment (urban renewal); (3) open space and urban land reserves; (4) public utilities; (5) community facilities, such as schools and hospitals; (6) new or expanded community development; (7) distressed areas; and (8) conservation, power and waterway developments.[20]

[18] *Ibid.*

[19] Letter from Advisory Commission on Intergovernmental Relations, Washington, D.C.: March 8, 1972.

[20] Derek Senior (ed.), *The Regional City, An Anglo-American Discussion of Metropolitan Planning* (Chicago: Aldine Publishing Co., 1966), p. 156.

The grant-in-aid is an important formal device for an intergovernmental manipulation of programs. These transfers of funds from one level of government to another come in different ways: (a) flat grants—requiring no matching funds; (b) proportionate grants—in proportion to a recipient's contribution to the program, taking need and capabilities into account; (c) percentage grants—on a fixed proportionate basis; (d) grants in kind—grants in goods. Additionally, fiscal subvention may occur in the form of tax offsets, shared revenues, and direct expenditures, such as to farmers, veterans, and college students. Not all grants adhere to the federal hierarchical structure, in that federal aid for such programs as urban renewal, housing, and airport construction, bypass the state authorities by direct outputs to the local level.[21]

> The Federal grant-in-aid is an important instrument for carrying out the partnership concept inherent in the federal system. It reconciles state and local administration of public services with Federal financial support in programs of national concern. Grants-in-aid, conditioned on performance requirements, make possible the achievement of national goals without overextending the Federal bureaucracy and without Federal assumption of state and local functions. By means of grants-in-aid, the Federal Government has not only been able to support existing state and local functions, but to stimulate the states and localities to expand their own programs and to undertake new ones.[22]

Regional planning institutions, albeit created by state enabling legislation, owe their development to federal fiscal invigoration; the federal government's conditional grants to local jurisdictions for area-wide planning devices have been catalytic to their growth. Although conditional grants-in-aid have not been utilized to induce governmental restructuring in urban areas, they have impelled comprehensive planning of the metropolis by area-wide planning agencies or councils of

---

[21] Elazar, "Federalism and Intergovernmental Relations," *op. cit.*
[22] *Metropolitan America: Challenge to Federalism, op. cit.,* p. 121.

government. This has been effected by predicating local governmental eligibility for aid upon a prior review of grant applications by an area-wide agency. The purpose of the requirement is to animate area-wide cooperation for coordinated decision making. The planning technique's ability to focus on the realities of region-wide problems would thereby provide the fragmented political system with an ordered process for metropolitan development.

So inured have the states and localities become to federal subvention, however, that they tend to be remiss in their financial contributions to the regional devices. Fiscal support of the area-wide councils by local jurisdictions is negligible. Only 26 percent of the regional councils receive state aid. Federal grants form the basis of the regional councils' budgets, accounting for 60 to 70 percent of their revenues amounting to approximately $40 million federal aid.[23]

Another important effect of federal grants-in-aid upon state and local policy is that they may influence action contrary to preferences at those levels. This occurs when a grant variates the marginal-cost pattern of the beneficiary unit. "By reducing the marginal cost of a new or an expanded program, a grant alters the political agenda by increasing the priority that that particular activity enjoys in that particular unit of government."[24] Accordingly, the alteration of the local political agenda may result in an expedient, but undesirable, new set of priorities.

The grant-in-aid also has a marginal-cost effect on local decision-making and local tax structures:

[23] The latest estimate of Federal aid to regional councils is approximately $40 million, although this data is difficult to determine because several programs require a State "pass through" of federal funds. Letter from National Association of Regional Councils, Washington, D.C., March 8, 1972; National Service to Regional Councils, *Key Federal Programs,* Special Report #7 (Washington, D.C.: July, 1968).

[24] Charles R. Adrian, "State and Local Government Participation in the Design and Administration of Intergovernmental Programs," in *Intergovernmental Realtions in the United States, op. cit ,* p. 39.

The marginal cost for the political decision-maker is less when he decides to finance a new program through a grant-in-aid or a shared tax rather than an increase in taxes by his unit of government. This is so because it is always more popular to be able to announce a new grant or shared tax from a higher level of government, than an increase in taxes by the unit of government served by the politician. This characteristic of the federal decision-making process discourages the diversification of taxes at the local level and the establishment of state taxes on an ability to pay basis; in particular it discourages steep graduation of state income taxes.[25]

Development of a Federal Urban Policy. Initial federal activities influencing urban physical development encouraged middle-income single-family dwelling construction, especially the suburban tract developments of large builders. This was done by the creation of the Home Loan Bank System (HLBS), in 1932, to sustain savings and loan institutions; and in 1934, the Federal Housing Administration (FHA) was established with the purpose of insuring home loans made by insurance companies and savings and commercial banks. Additionally, a small-scale low rent public housing program was initiated.[26] The intent of these programs, however, was primarily to stimulate the depressed construction industry and financial institutions, rather than to affect an urban development pattern.

Prompted by a postwar housing shortage, the federal government passed a Housing Act in 1949[27] that called for a program of clearing and rebuilding of obsolescent portions of the central cities into new housing areas. This emphasis on urban redevelopment was limited to existing areas of predominantly residential land-uses, or areas intended for residential purposes. The Housing and Home Finance Agency (HHFA) was established to coordinate activities on behalf of the program. The Act's focus on the physical im-

---

[25] *Ibid.*, p. 40.
[26] Rodwin, *op. cit.*
[27] *Ibid.*

provement of the cities through the use of the bulldozer, strove to enhance the cities' attractiveness to dwellers and thus to improve their competitive posture *vis à vis* the suburbs. Consequently, the Housing Act of 1949 was in direct contradiction to the FHA's stimulation of centrifugal development.

There was a perceptible transition from urban redevelopment to urban renewal in the 1954 amendments to the Housing Act.[28] Although clearance was to be continued in the worst slums and in designated areas where there was anticipation of significant effects, the thrust of the amended Act was on areal conservation and rehabilitation. In effect, the concept of redevelopment was altered by providing inducements to local authorities and private capital to improve existing housing conditions.

There were some additional notable features in the 1954 Act.[29] Section 221 invigorated the development of low rent housing for renewal-dislodged families by authorizing the FHA to insure loans for the construction of these units either on or off renewal sites. The 1949 restriction of non-residential redevelopment to 10 percent of the affected area was expanded to 35 percent. The Act initiated a federal concern for planning by including the requirement of a "Workable Program" as a criterion for grant eligibility. The "workable programs" consisted of the formulation of neighborhood studies, long-range land use plans, and financial and administrative preparations for their fulfillment. Finally, Section 701 authorized matching grants to underwrite state, metropolitan, and regional planning studies for urban renewal guidance. On the whole, the stress of the 1954 Act was on the rehabilitation of the inner cities, with rent subsidies and private management opted over the earlier programs of large-scale redevelopment and public housing, albeit with a helpful provision for the latter.

A metropolitan perspective emerged in 1955 with a new public facilities loan program administered by the Community Facilities Administration of the HHFA. This program was the first instance of federal encouragement of comprehensive

[28] *Ibid.*
[29] *Ibid.*

planned development through a regional framework. It provided, in addition to interest-free advances for preliminary public works planning, the incentive of federal matching grants for the creation of state, metropolitan, and regional planning agencies to engage in comprehensive studies of metropolitan or regional areas.

Once the federal government approved of the metropolis as the proper unit for land use planning, it would follow with a series of purposive legislation for the effectuation of orderly regional development.[30] This was to begin in 1961, when as a condition for receiving federal loans for the acquisition and improvement of mass transportation facilities, localities had to provide for area-wide comprehensive transportation planning. Later, Congress authorized enlarged grants

> . . . and extended [these] policies to public works, recreational areas, beautification programs, advance land acquisition, and large-scale land management—but always with a proviso or an incentive for area-wide planning agencies.[31]

The 1965 Amendment to the Housing Act of 1954 launched a federal program of energizing organizations of public officials in metropolitan areas by making them eligible to receive grants for the preparation of comprehensive metropolitan plans.

The Housing and Home Finance Agency's "Planning Agency Letter Number 50" issued in 1965, outlined the program's rationale:

> The main objective of these grants is to foster metropolitan cooperation on a broad front by establishing and maintaining organizations of policy and decision-makers representing the various local governments within metropolitan areas. Such organizations are viewed as effective forums for studying and resolving issues raised by metropolitan problems, or the preparation of metropolitan

---

[30] *Ibid.;* Anthony H. Anderson, "The Movement Towards Regional Government," (unpublished Master's thesis, Department of Government, Claremont Graduate School, Claremont, Calif., 1970).

[31] Rodwin, *op. cit.,* pp. 246–247.

comprehensive plans, for developing action programs for carrying out metropolitan comprehensive plans, and for determining regional policies affecting governmental and functional activities.

The growing importance of urban issues in the affairs of the nation led to the elevation of the HHFA to a cabinet-level Department of Housing and Urban Development (HUD). The new Department was organized into five functional divisions reflecting its perspectives and priorities. Urban renewal, relocation, low-rent public housing, neighborhood facilities, and social services formed one division. Mortgage credit became another. A third division was responsible for the requirements of metropolitan areas, such as planning for public facilities. Urban projects demonstrations and experiments, and intergovernmental relations were placed in a fourth division. The fifth integrated the other divisions because of its concentration on information systems for management and policy planning, and for program assessment.

The reorganization of HUD reinforced changes in urban development policy which had occurred over the past decade. It deemphasized housing as such and stressed instead urban and metropolitan perspectives, intergovernmental relationships, and significant development tools. Still unclear, however, were the actual strategies in behalf of which the new administrative machinery was to be deployed.[32]

In 1966, the Demonstration Cities and Metropolitan Development Act sought to convert area-wide planning from a didactic exercise to an advisory function with some power. Accordingly, Section 204 of the new legislation specified that an area-wide planning agency had to review all applications of local governments for federal aid for development projects.[33] The reviewing body—

---

[32] *Ibid.,* pp. 250–251.

[33] Eligible projects for federal assistance: "airports, highways, hospitals, libraries, open space land projects, sewage facilities and waste treatment plants, transportation facilities, water development

> . . . which is, to the greatest practicable extent, composed of or responsible to the elected officials of a unit of area-wide government or by the units of general local governments within whose jurisdiction such agency is authorized to engage in such planning . . .[34]

was then to comment to a coordinating federal agency on the compatibility of the proposed project to the area's comprehensive plan.

> There was a complementary requirement that "where projects [were] proposed by local special-purpose bodies, such as sewer commissions or park authorities, the proposal [had to] be submitted for comment to the county, municipality, or other unit of general local government having jurisdiction over the project areas." There were even special supplementary grants to ensure coordinated scheduling of the land use, financial, and operational plans for development throughout the region.[35]

The Act authorized the Bureau of the Budget to administer the "review-and-comment" provision of Section 204. Thus, in 1967 the Bureau certified 171 metropolitan planning commissions and councils of governments as the area-wide reviewing agencies for development grant applications from the local jurisdictions in their areas.[36]

The Intergovernmental Cooperation Act of 1968 was designed to add state agencies to the review and comment process, with the Bureau of the Budget specified as the Act's administrator. The new legislation inaugurated a new procedural level—the State Clearinghouse, an agency designated by the Governor—to insure that local development

---

and land conservation projects, and water supply and distribution facilities." Joseph F. Zimmerman (ed.), *1968 Metropolitan Area Annual* (Albany, N.Y.: Graduate School of Public Affairs, State University of New York at Albany, 1967), p. 59.

[34] *Ibid.*, p. 62.
[35] Rodwin, *op. cit.*, p. 247.
[36] Zimmerman, *op. cit.*

projects be not only consistent with area-wide plans, but with state-wide plans as well. The creation of a state clearinghouse has permitted policy-makers and planners at the state level to have a clear focus of all proposed and actual development activities undertaken within their state.

The Bureau of the Budget was now overseeing a fully mobilized federal system on behalf of coordinated urban planning, insofar as federal legislation—Demonstration Cities and Metropolitan Development Act of 1966, and Intergovernmental Cooperation Act of 1968—have provided for a hierarchy of advisory clearinghouses for federal assistance applications. The Bureau outlined the coordination process to all involved agencies in its Circular No. A-95:

> This Circular furnishes guidance to Federal agencies for added cooperation with states and local governments in the evaluation, review, and coordination of Federal assistance programs and projects. The Circular promulgates regulations which provide, in part, for:
> a. Encouraging the establishment of a project notification and review system to facilitate coordinated development planning on an intergovernmental basis for certain Federal assistance programs in furtherance of Section 204 of the Demonstration Cities and Metropolitan Development Act of 1966, and Title IV of the Intergovernmental Cooperation Act of 1968.
> b. Notification, upon request, of Governors and State legislatures of grants-in-aid made under Federal programs in each State pursuant to Section 201 of the Intergovernmental Cooperation Act of 1968.
> c. Coordination of Federal development programs and projects with State, regional, and local development planning pursuant to Title IV of the Intergovernmental Cooperation Act of 1968.[37]

Subsequently, the Bureau of the Budget, by authority of the National Environmental Policy Act of 1969, added a requirement for an "Environmental Impact Statement" as part of the application for federal development grants.

---

[37] Executive Office of the President, Bureau of the Budget, Circular No. A-95, Washington, D.C., July 24, 1969.

It is the intent of the federal government to [now] include environmental consideration as an integral part in the evaluation of applications. Applications should be evaluated in terms of whether advantages to the public in proceeding with the project in question outweigh the disadvantages to the environment.[38]

The State Clearinghouse's function in this regard is to insure that the subordinate clearinghouse levels have complied with the exigency of an Environmental Impact Statement, or furnish its own statement.

The federal government's answer to the deterioration of the central cities was displayed in the passage of the Demonstration Cities and Metropolitan Development Act of 1966, and the ensuing Housing and Urban Development Act of 1968. While the 1965 Housing Act focused on loan insurance for the purchase and improvement of large-scale subdivisions, the 1966 Act emphasized a broader scope of community development, to the extent of encompassing whole metropolitan areas, albeit still within the context of loan insuring devices. The 1968 Act, however, sought to exploit the bond rather than the mortgage market, and thereby attract more ample private investment for more expansive development. The legislation's aim was to stimulate the development of new towns to accommodate the projected vast increases of population, and to provide for suburban outlets for central city minorities.

[The] Congress expressly grappled with the problem of heavy fixed charges during the development period when the ["new town"] project earned no income. To help overcome this difficulty, the 1968 law provided for federally guaranteed cash-flow debentures which would be large enough to cover major costs (site acquisition, site improvement, construction, and fixed charges) until the development could generate income from the sale of lots, houses and nonresidential properties. The law also authorized a small amount of supplementary grants to encourage the

[38] Memorandum from Lieutenant Governor Ed Reinecke, California State Clearinghouse, Office of Intergovernmental Management, June 18, 1970 (mimeographed).

use, in connection with the new communities, of existing federal grant programs for water, sewer, and open space projects.[39]

Goal-Seeking Performance of the State Governments

After many years of unsympathetic treatment of urban problems, the states are beginning to exercise a political leverage affecting metropolitan development. This, after a protracted period of functional isolation caused by the unequal apportionment of State legislatures, which fostered a direct communion between metropolitan officials and a more responsive Congress and national executive branch. Despite an awakening at the state level to the range of urban programs and the states' legal responsibility to assist local governments in metropolitan areas, the state governments have been functionally handicapped. A history of government dominated by rural squirearchies—now becoming government with a suburban predominance—and constitutional restrictions and financial inadequacy have restricted the responsiveness of the states. But these disadvantages notwithstanding, the states possess a legal hegemony over the local jurisdictions, and a capability for raising more revenue than they have heretofore, to exercise responsible leadership over their dominion.

The case for strong State participation in metropolitan affairs is thus based not only on the State's legal powers and capacity to raise revenue from metropolitanwide sources, but also on its unique vantage point. State technical assistance as well as financial aid is warranted, not because technical expertise is lacking at the local level but because a centralized grasp of areawide problems is likely to be lacking. As for financial aid, the Federal government has undertaken many problems of direct local grants to which most States make no contribution at all. If "States responsibilities as well as States rights" is not to be an empty slogan, State government must accept the principle that taxpayers of the State have a greater responsibility than taxpayers of the Nation in financing local

[39] Rodwin, *op. cit.*, pp. 257–258.

government activities within the State. Extending Federal aid to local governments while the respective States stand idly by is incompatible with the philosophy of the federal system.[40]

In addition to their responsibilities for education, health, and highways, their considerable regulatory powers, and their service as a conduit for several federal grant-in-aid programs, the states have the wherewithal, in terms of policy output, to respond to the needs of metropolitan areas. These policy outputs can be categorized into six general areas for purposes of examination: (1) attitudes of the state executives; (2) legislative action; (3) state agency involvement; (4) state agency coordination; (5) state planning; and (6) state financial assistance.[41]

Most state chief executives were sensitized to the increasing concentration of votes in urban areas before the state legislatures, and they have gone on record as favoring regional cooperation and coordination for the strengthening of the local governments and the states. The record of state legislative enactments on behalf of these pronouncements falls short of gubernatorial rhetoric.

Legislative action regarding the formation of area-wide devices can be analyzed from several perspectives:

> . . . legislation dealing with interlocal agreement or joint exercise of powers, transfer of local government activities or functions, the creation and organization of regional councils of governments, and the creation of regional special or multi-purpose districts and authorities.[42]

Interlocal agreements have become *de rigueur* in many states, and state legislatures are providing formal authorization for their formation, legitimacy, and longevity. Interlocal agreements or contracts seem to be preferred to the alterna-

---

[40] *Metropolitan America: Challenge to Federalism, op. cit.,* pp. 118–119.

[41] National Service to Regional Councils, "Regional Councils and the States," Special Report #8, Washington, D.C., November, 1968.

[42] *Ibid.,* p. 3.

tive of a transfer of functions that would entail the re-
linquishment of some power to another authority and thus
affect the basis of home rule. Only three states have enabling
legislation providing for some aspect of transfer of functions.
Forty-three states have legislation catering to some form of
regional planning mechanism; thirty-nine of these have broad-
based permissive legislation, with the remaining states providing each new agency with specific legislation.

Councils of government, although a recent intergovernmental innovation, have proliferated ever since the 1965
Housing Act furnished a financial stimulus for their development. Generally, state governments have not kept up with
their growth rate, with just nine states, enacting enabling
legislation for their formation. Many of the councils have re-
sorted to other legal techniques, such as broad interlocal agreements or the non-profit corporation, for their establishment.
In 1968, twenty-five states had enabling legislation for specific
purpose districts or authorities, such as general service districts,
metropolitan transit districts, airport authorities, water pollution control or water conservation districts, air quality control
districts, and the like. However, there is a dearth of enabling
legislation for the creation of multipurpose and regional authorities.[43]

Animated by the Demonstration Cities and Metropolitan
Development Act of 1966 and the Intergovernmental Cooperation Act of 1968, the states have been establishing
agencies to deal with the needs and problems of the localities.
In 1972 there were approximately thirty states with active
agencies for community or local affairs and several others con-
sidering the formation of such functions. The methods of creating these agencies vary, and have included executive orders or
legislative statutes, among others. The functions of an agency
for local affairs differ from state to state, but commonly encompass advice and information to local governments, planning and area development, research and publication, coordination of state and federal grants-in-aid, promotion of

[43] *Ibid.*

interlocal cooperation, and training programs for local officials. There are agencies that have budgets in excess of $20 million, notably the Connecticut Department of Community Affairs with a two-year budget of $55 million, and the Washington Planning and Community Affairs Agency which, in 1968, distributed $25 million for direct aid to the localities.[44]

The agencies with large budgets generally have some administrative control over state grant disbursement to the local jurisdictions. The Connecticut agency, for example, allocated its budget to eighteen new programs in such areas as planning and zoning, physical improvements and community development, housing, and human resource development. As a condition of eligibility for this financial aid, the localities are required to prepare comprehensive "community development action plans."[45] Most agencies for community affairs, however, have budgets ranging from $100,000 to $3 million, although there is a trend toward increasing fiscal resources. Many of the agencies are also recipients of substantial federal matching funds.[46]

The states have long been plagued with a lack of agency coordination attributable to the phenomenon of "functional government"—autonomous hierarchies of specialized functional authorities—and a fragmented and confused pattern of channeling of funds to various localities.

The Bureau of the Budget, in light of this need for cooperation and coordination on a regional basis, has emphasized the need for dividing the states into one specific set of planning and development regions. These regions are to serve as a basis for comprehensive social, economic and physical resources planning and development activities, and as a basis for coordination between state-wide and regional planning, development and services.[47]

[44] Zimmerman, *op. cit.;* "Regional Councils and the States," *op. cit.*
[45] Zimmerman, *op. cit.,* p. 47.
[46] "Regional Councils and the States," *op. cit.*
[47] *Ibid.,* p. 6.

In response to the federal agency's stress, thirty-one states complied by delineating areas suitable for regional planning. However, only twenty of these states formalized the territorial designations through executive orders, or legislation, or some other official means, while the remainder simply indicated areas appropriate for regional planning organizations.

Each state [with an officially designated district] is utilizing these districts in some state-level planning activities; yet the pattern and areas of coordination vary in each state. States have coordinated their activities with the substate areas in relation to: area-wide planning, local planning assistance, water resource planning, mental health planning, health services, public information services, etc. The extent of involvement and number of programs involved in this coordination will undoubtedly continue to grow in the future.[48]

The need for an effective intergovernmental coordination process has caused an interest in horizontal and vertical urban information systems, to enable the local jurisdictions, the regional agencies, and the states, working cooperatively, to have joint access to comprehensive and timely data. Accordingly, the Lockheed Missiles and Space Company completed, in 1965, a study commissioned by the State of California on the feasibility of such a systems network. The study recommended the

> . . . development and implementation of a State-wide Federated Information System (SFIS) at a cost of about $100 million over a ten-year period. The term "federated" arose from the concept of separate computer installations in state departments and in local governments, all tied together by a communications network, with a central computer to act as the switching and translating mechanisms.[49]

[48] *Ibid.*

[49] Joel M. Kibbee, "The Scope of Large-Scale Computer-Based System in Governmental Functions," *Governing Urban Society: New Scientific Approaches,* Stephen B. Sweeney and James C. Charlesworth, (eds.) Monograph 7 (Philadelphia: The American Academy of Political and Social Science, May, 1967).

Although the legislature subsequently provided the necessary funds for the initial design of the system, the SFIS has yet to be fully implemented because of controversy over its feasibility, particularly in view of the nonexistence of standards and the incongruity of data across department lines and between echelons of government. The State of California continues to underwrite systems feasibility studies, an example of which was the California Regional Land Use Information System completed in 1967. The study used Santa Clara County as the demonstration area, and analyzed

> . . . land-use data as it exists, is used, or needed throughout the state, for any or all departments and agencies of the state, local units of governments, and federal agencies operating within the state.[50]

While there is an absence of fully integrated state-wide information systems, counties and councils of government are utilizing sophisticated computers and some are even in the process of developing integrated collections of applications information systems. In the San Francisco Bay Area, for example,

> . . . in addition to the separate counties—such as Alameda, Santa Clara, and San Francisco, all of which have elaborate information system plans—and projects such as the land-use study . . . , the Bay Area Transportation Study Commission as a necessary consequence of its long-range transportation planning mission, [had] implemented a fairly sophisticated information system and established a useful and well-documented data base. The Association of Bay Area Governments (ABAG) [had] the responsibility for acting as the intermediary which [furnished] data from this data base to public agencies in the area. And ABAG is also sponsoring the Bay Area Automated Information System Coordinating Committee (BAAISCC), which is concerned with the possible establishment of an area-wide information service in the Bay Area.[51]

[50] *Ibid.*, p. 192.
[51] *Ibid.*, p. 195.

The increase in the states' concern with urban issues and regional activities has generated an impetus, in some states, for more generous financial subvention to subordinate levels. Some states now provide aid, matching funds for federal grants, and conditional grants for special projects, but, in 1968, only seven states had programs of direct financial and administrative assistance to regional agencies. Connecticut, Texas, and Washington are three of the seven.[52]

Goal-oriented Execution of the Federal System

Despite the existence of adequate machinery and models of productive collaboration, intergovernmental execution is, nonetheless, functionally victimized by dysjunctions and frictions within the federal system. Basic to the malfunctioning of coordinated effort is the system's political and fiscal fragmentation which often accounts for disorderly, uneconomic, and antisocial patterns of urban development and allocations of resources. The intergovernmental experience is too frequently a pattern of anarchic competition and parochial selfishness at the local level; a state government unwilling to challenge the status quo of home rule, and indifferent to urban financial and service needs; and a Federal role beset with policy contradictions.

> On the one hand, Congress enacts area-wide planning requirements, strengthens representative regional bodies, adopts programs to assist the rehabilitation of central cities. On the other hand, the Federal-State highway program, FHA's activities, the failure of a fair and uniform relocation policy, and various location decisions of the Department of Defense and other Federal agencies more often than not have collided head on with long term urban development needs.[53]

Factors in intergovernmental abrasiveness are tensions between political and administrative actors; and the states'

[52] "Regional Councils and the States," *op. cit.*
[53] Advisory Commission on Intergovernmental Relations, *Urban America and the Federal System, Commission Findings and Proposals,* M-47 (Washington, D.C.: October, 1969), p. 2.

inconsistent functional performances with concomitant disparities in bureaucratic professionalism within the federal framework. The functional incompatability between the bureaucracy and the legislatures is centered on their differences in values, interests, and constituencies.

> . . . [While] the bureaucrat is maximizing professional values in the decision-making process, the legislator at all levels is maximizing grass-roots values. Congressmen and even United States Senators have essentially parochial views to protect in the process.[54]

The states' role in the federal system has often been minimized by urban and federal administrators, with common policy making focuses, short-circuiting rural-dominated state governments. The pre-*Baker* v. *Carr* apportionment practices heavily favoring small town values and life styles, have insulated many state legislatures from the urban environment and deterred a professionalization of their bureaucracies. Consequently, urban administrators frustrated by indifference and ineffectuality at the state level, have tended to deal directly with Washington. Reapportionment in many states has not produced a big-city legislative predominance. The new pattern of representation in state governments has adhered to the new demographic realities and provides a proportionate voice to urban interests—interests now dichotomized along city-suburban lines.

With local governments unwilling or unable to respond to metropolitan problems, it has become increasingly necessary for the federal and state governments to assume greater dominance in urban affairs. The federal government's role development has been inevitable because of the influences and conditions causing a centripetal focus on policy-making and governmental controls. The energizing of the states is vital to the perpetuation of the federal system, because prolonged functional immobility of the states creates the suspicion of their anachronism and thus, the pretext for their extinction.

[54] Adrian, *op. cit.*, p. 37.

Some who have discussed metropolitan organization seem to suggest that one day the State governments will wither away, replaced by areal distributions of power on a regional basis . . . Since the State is influential, it makes sense to turn it into an instrument of benefit to more efficient regional development instead of plotting its elimination. . . .[55]

[55] U.S., Congress, Senate, Subcommittee on Intergovernmental Relations of the Committee on Government Operations, in Cooperation with the Joint Center for Urban Studies of the Massachusetts Institute of Technology and Harvard University, *The Effectiveness of Metropolitan Planning,* 88th Cong., 2d Sess., 1964, pp. 30–31.

V

Planning and the City

Community Planning

PLANNING SEEKS the orderly and rational development
of a community through anticipation and foresight,
involving sequential problem-solving over time.[1]
Planning arose out of a sense of failure of market
forces and of private and political actions in fulfilling the
public interest. While the public's interest is oftentimes an
illusory condition, in planning terms it is becoming more and
more synonymous with satisfactory living conditions to which
purpose the social, economic and physical elements are syn-
thesized. Thus, community planning becomes an instrument
for the guidance of growth and development on behalf of improving the needs and the facets of the living environment.
In this manner, community planning comes "close to the art
of life itself."[2]

[1] Herbert L. Marx, Jr. (ed.), *Community Planning, The Reference Shelf,* Vol. 28, No. 4 (New York: W. W. Wilson Company,
1956).
[2] Percival and Paul Goodman, *Communitas, Means of Livelihood and Ways of Life* (New York: Vintage Books, 1960), p. 17.

A city, a civilization's microcosm, is the reflection of the civilization itself. Planning in a democratic society is an acutely complex task because of a multiplicity of competing interests and groups and the decentralization of government.

> If a major object of our existence were to create great cities of beauty and grace there would be something to be said in favor of dictatorship. As a rule, the great cities of the past have been the cities of the powerful city-states in which a dominant king or governing body had the power and the will to impose its land-use structures upon an obedient populace. Weak or divided local governments, responsive to the push and pressure of the heterogeneous interest groups which make up a city, have rarely managed to intervene enough to prevent the unpalatable kind of growth which typifies our larger American urban areas.[3]

The most serious barrier to planning is the fear of governmental power by the American people.[4] But there are a number of functions the citizens recognize to be within the proper sphere of government, and so long as they adhere to the non-controversial realm allowed by custom and acceptance, planners "do not risk being charged with socialistic or dictatorial tendencies."[5] Proper tasks for planning interest are (1) the street system; (2) parking and traffic; (3) public buildings; (4) public health and safety; (5) schools; (6) zoning; (7) recreation; (8) subdivision regulations; (9) land use; (10) characteristics of population analysis; and (11) finance.[6] Ultimately, the public most fully legitimizes planning's use of public power when it enhances the private interest sector. Land use policy, zoning, and building

---

[3] Raymond Vernon, "The Myth and Reality of Our Urban Problems," *City and Suburb, The Economics of Metropolitan Growth,* Benjamin Chinitz, (ed.) (Englewood Cliffs, N.J.: Prentice-Hall, Inc., 1964), p. 97.

[4] Alan Altschuler, *The City Planning Process, A Political Analysis* (Ithaca, N.Y.: Cornell University Press, Cornell Paperbacks, 1969).

[5] *Ibid.,* pp. 361–362.

[6] Marx (ed.), *op. cit.,* p. 61.

codes[7] that stimulate private investment and development, are the activities best received, and planning has been responsive to this prevalent ethos by utilizing techniques to facilitate capital investment. Zoning code enforcement, the use of tax policy as a mechanism for influencing the pattern of land use through the market mechanism, and the exercise of eminent domain as an eventual stimulus to redevelopment and capital improvement, have all been used successfully to that end.[8]

Not all planners singlemindedly pursue the popular private ethos. Some formulate plans with social ramifications, inspired solely by public considerations. Many of these formulations, however, are purely speculative and visionary as political realities in most areas foreclose the implementation of controversial schemes. Planners, nonetheless, are showing some interest in generating public participation in planning agencies—"advocacy" planning[9]—or in collaborating with the public—through dialogues and in actively seeking out public values and life styles in order for plans to conform to these —with the public as the planners' client.[10]

More far-reaching, and purely speculative, was the Goodmans' discussion of planning new communities which can either conform to a society's life style and ethos or shape it through spatial form.[11] The latter formulation was introduced as a proposed refinement of the New Towns concept— originated by Ebenzer Howard with his Garden City of the nineteenth century—and contemplates the actual development of new communities, in the United States and in Great Britain, to suit a society's "personality" while attempting to

---

[7] Building codes and zoning specifications have the effect of raising property values in some suburbs with the intent of discouraging a heterogeneity in the population.

[8] Chinitz (ed.), *op. cit.*

[9] Paul Davidoff, "Advocacy and Pluralism in Planning," *Taming Megalopolis,* Vol. II, *How to Manage an Urbanized World,* H. Wentworth Eldredge, (ed.) (Garden City, N.Y.: Anchor Books, Doubleday and Co., Inc., 1967).

[10] David R. Godschalk, "The Circle of Urban Participation," in Eldredge (ed.), Vol. II, *op. cit.*

[11] Goodman, *op. cit.*

improve living conditions. The Goodmans proposed three community models: (1) the City of Efficient Consumption—to emphasize high production, a high standard of living, and artificially induced demand, or in other words, a city "drawn from the tastes and drives of America";[12] (2) a New Community bereft of difference between production and consumption—a community of style and refined work and a great deal of personal interdependence; and (3) a community of "Planned Security with minimum regulation"—with state directed centers of labor to which all citizens, for a period of their lives, must belong, and a life-style and economic sector whose *raison d'etre* is efficiency.

The Planning Experience

Despite early America's intellectual bias against urban life,[13] urban planning in America was born with William Penn's Philadelphia and its gridiron of streets, Pierre Charles L'Enfant's grandiose plan of Washington, and General Oglethorpe's Savannah.[14] But these were the early exceptions, and so

> . . . the story of city planning truly begins with the ugliness, noise, and filth of the new industrial cities, their lack of fresh air and recreation space, the steady growth of their slums, and the devastation of the surrounding countryside.[15]

It was then that Ebenezer Howard, in 1898, proposed his "Garden City" as a balanced urban environment

> . . . that would combine the social and cultural facilities of the city with the closeness to nature of the village . . . "Town and country," wrote Howard, "must

[12] *Ibid.*

[13] As exemplified by Thomas Jefferson's view of great cities ". . . as pestilential to the morals, the health, and the liberties of man."

[14] Harland Bartholomew, "History of Planning," in Marx (ed.), *op. cit.*

[15] Frank Fisher, "Where City Planning Stands Today," in Marx (ed.), *op. cit.,* p. 86.

be married, and out of this union will spring a new life, a new hope, a new civilization."[16]

However, unlike today's suburbs, Howard envisioned a community balanced in terms of home, industry, and market and likewise of political, social, and recreational functions.[17]

The blight of industrial cities prompted the emergence in the early twentieth century of the "City Beautiful Movement" led by community notables who sought to implement their aesthetic values in grand civic centers, throughfares, and parks. The Movement was, however, more noted for its rhetoric than for its achievements, and in the 1920's gave way to the "City Efficient" which concentrated on competence in transport and public works.[18] Modern city planning has utilized some of the techniques of engineering and economics, among others, to promote the "efficient functioning of the city." Planning, too, has now become a key governmental procedure for arranging a physical pattern through the manipulation of land-use controls. Recently, however, the planning vision has been expanded to include the myriad complexities of urban interactions and, consequently, its focus has begun to encompass socio-economic and political, as well as physical, elements that act in the shaping of the functioning and development of urban settlements.[19]

Planning is an eclectic art that derives expertise from many disciplines capable of contributing to a city plan. For example, the civil engineer is concerned with water supply, sewers, storm drainage, utilities, streets, transportation, and terminals; the sociologist with housing, population density,

[16] *Ibid.*

[17] The first large-scale attempt to implement Howard's ideas was in Britain under the New Town Act of 1946. His balanced community had to wait for the new forms of transportation and power sources to make decentralized light industries attractive and possible.

[18] James G. Coke, "Antecedents of Local Planning," *Principles and Practices of Urban Planning,* William I. Goodman and Eric C. Freund, (eds.) (Washington, D.C.: International City Managers Association, Municipal Management Series, 1968).

[19] Harvey S. Perloff, *Education for Planning: City, State and Regional* (Baltimore: The Johns Hopkins Press, 1957), pp. 11–12.

and parks and recreation facilities; the architect with buildings, both public and private, and open spaces; the economist
with trends in employment and the volume and type of
business and industrial activity.[20] All of these experts, and
more, are needed as partners in the making of a rational and
improved urban environment.

The planner should try to understand the effect
technology has on living, and to adapt the physical form
of the city accordingly. The automobile, the airplane, the
radio and television and atomic fusion have changed the
mode of living profoundly, yet we are biologically the same
creatures and require much the same as we always have
in the ways of quiet, relaxation, family association, friends.
The planner's job is to fit the old essential needs into a
framework that will take care of the new mechanism, so
that we can go from one to the other . . . It is up to the
physical planner to provide ways by which the opposing
requirements of our time can be, if not reconciled, at least
brought into some sane relation with each other.[21]

Planning is expected to consistently be responsive to
considerations relating to social and economic development as
well as to the physical environment. Planning is endeavoring
to focus on ways and means to enlarge the scope of human opportunities and well-being by ameliorating the urban environment and aiding in its economic development.[22] City planners
are, moreover, acutely aware of the fiscal and cultural crises
besetting the central cities as a result of the flight of productive middle-and-upper-class elements. This has not only
caused a serious shrinkage in city tax bases but has produced
a degradation in social and political life, and in aesthetic
surroundings. Yet, despite these losses the demands and expenditures for city services have been steadily rising as ne-

[20] Harland Bartholomew, "Elements of the City Plan," in Marx
(ed.), op. cit., p. 82.
[21] Henry S. Churchill, "Planning in a Free Society," in Marx
(ed.), op. cit., p. 82.
[22] City Government For the Future, Report of the Los Angeles
City Charter Commission, City Hall, Los Angeles, California, July,
1969.

cessitated by increased emphasis on fire, police, welfare, education, and the like, in view of the changing composition of the city's population.[23] Suburban areas, too, are often faced with fiscal shortages, as their tax bases are oftentimes inadequate to support a full complement of services. With these problems in mind the American Institute of Planners, in October, 1962, issued their "Statement on Responsibility of the Planner":

> . . . first, the planner investigates, describes, synthesizes, analyzes and evaluates the overall problems and conditions of the urban area; . . . second, the planner predicts or estimates changes and trends, evaluates needs, considers alternatives and recommends practices for action by his community client.[24]

Hence, a local planning program should be so structured as best to meet the community's needs and to include the following seven functions:

1. Establishment of community development objectives.
2. Conduct of research on growth and development of the city.
3. The making of development plans and programs.
4. Effort aimed at increasing public understanding and acceptance of planning.
5. Providing of technical service to other governmental agencies and private groups.
6. Coordination of development activities affecting city growth.
7. The administration of land use controls (zoning and subdivision regulations).[25]

The functions are performed in a way so as to ultimately influence community decision-makers in their policies involving

[23] Edward C. Banfield and James Q. Wilson, *City Politics* (New York: Vintage Books, 1963).
[24] Richard F. Babcock, *The Zoning Game, Municipal Practices and Policies* (Madison, Wis.: The University of Wisconsin Press, 1969), p. 66.
[25] James H. Pickford, "The Local Planning Agency: Organization and Structure," in Goodman and Freund (eds.), *op. cit.,* p. 526.

the environment. A planning agency's activities[26] are properly allocated to various time-ranges (long, middle, short) and space-scales (metropolitan, county, city, district, project) to fit the appropriate areas of endeavor. Time ranges are selected on the basis of efficient administration, rationality, and degrees of complexity, comprehensiveness and scale of projects. Long range planning, requiring a futuristic analysis of from 15 to 50 years, includes the preparation, review, and maintenance of a "comprehensive" plan.[27] A planning agency, in this time range, may also cooperate in metropolitan or regional studies and planning. Middle range planning, preparation for actions taking effect in from two to ten years, must include capital improvement programming, zoning studies, and renewal studies. Short-range planning, consisting of the agency's daily business, usually involves zoning administration, urban renewal projects, public division control and occasional controls over "civic" art.[28] The planning agency also oversees work, related to planning, performed by other agencies.

Comprehensive Plan

A comprehensive plan is an official public document adopted by a local government as a policy guide to decisions about the physical development in the community. It indicates in a general way how the leaders of the government want the community to develop in the next 20 to 30 years.[29]

This set of maps and policy statements comprises the proposed guidelines for a community's long range development. It naturally affects the potential physical development to include the uses of land—private and public—the environmental aesthet-

[26] "Many of the activities are mandatory—that is, they are usually imposed by statute, charter, or ordinance; others, though not so formalized, are customary and necessary." *Ibid.*, p. 546.

[27] The comprehensive plan is also sometimes called the "general" or "master" plan.

[28] Pickford, "The Local Planning Agency," in Goodman and Freund (eds.), *op. cit.*

[29] Alan Black, "The Comprehensive Plan," in Goodman and Freund (eds.), *op. cit.*

ics, and capital improvements. But its far-reaching and comprehensive aspect may also influence the spatial pattern of life, the growth potential, and the social environment of the community.

The strength of the comprehensive plan as a technique derives from the perspective it gives of the inter-relationships between functional, time and spatial components of urban development. In a functional context, it provides an overview of the structural relationships among land use, transportation, and community facilities and services. In a time context, it provides for sequence or scheduled progression of public action in relation to urban expansion, and in a spatial context it establishes the pattern and form of urban expansion.[30]

Thus, the comprehensive plan is an inclusive, general policy statement which, while focused on physical development is related to community goals and social and economic policies.[31]

The concept of the comprehensive plan received its impetus from the federal influence upon local communities to formulate long-range goals for their development. There were few meaningful comprehensive plans until the Housing and Redevelopment Act of 1949 "encouraged the cities to undertake vast new projects that would require planning and it agreed to pay much of the cost of planning."[32] The Housing and Redevelopment Act of 1954, amended the 1949 Act, and created the "701" program providing matching funds to local governments for comprehensive planning.[33] It also made a "workable" community program a prerequisite for grants which became available for public housing, open space, and regional (or metropolitan) planning programs.[34]

It is increasingly evident however, that for a planning policy to become effective "public and private development

[30] F. Stuart Chapin, Jr., "Existing Techniques of Shaping Urban Growth," in Eldredge (ed.), Vol. II, *op. cit.*, p. 731.

[31] Black, *op. cit.*

[32] Banfield and Wilson, *op. cit.*, p. 191.

[33] Black, *op. cit.*

[34] Banfield and Wilson, *op. cit.*

action must be coordinated within a framework of comprehensive development policy."[35] Unplanned, opportunistic growth and development are endemic to many urban areas and have reaped negative environmental, economic and social results. Planning in a democratic society must, of course, await the pleasure of community consensus and political legitimization for consequent implementation. Planning is thus subject to the nuances and interchanges of the political system in which it exists. But a planned city is the mark of our civilization just as a Gothic Cathedral or Roman aqueduct were expressions of earlier civilizations. Edmund Bacon in his introduction to "Design of Cities" underscores this clearly:

> The form of the city always has been and always will be a pitiless indicator of the state of man's civilization. This form is determined by the multiplicity of decisions made by the people who live in it. In certain circumstances these decisions have interacted to produce a force of such clarity and form that a noble city has been born . . . My hope is to dispel the idea, so widely and uncritically held, that cities are a kind of grand accident, beyond the control of the human will, and that they respond only to some immutable law. I contend that human will can be exercised effectively on our cities now, so that the form that they take will be a true expression of the highest aspirations of our civilization. . . .[36]

Planning Efficiency

Transportation Systems. The concern for an adequate and efficient transportation system, a middle time range objective, is directly connected with an area's growth and development. If the planner's task is to bolster the economic advantages and minimize the economic shortcomings of a city, then traffic flow must be managed to achieve this end. Affluence in

[35] James Pickford, "The Local Planning Agency," in Goodman and Freund (eds.), *op. cit.,* p. 527.
[36] U.S., Congress, House, *Building the American City, Report of the National Commission on Urban Problems to the Congress and to the President of the United States,* 91st Cong., 1st Sess., December 12, 1968, House Doc. No. 91–23.

an area compounds the transportation problem, as higher incomes lead to more automobiles resulting in more congestion, the need for more roads and freeways and a demand for more land space. Downtown interests, in an effort to salvage that area's role as the center of metropolitan flows of goods, services, and people, insist that the city's economic development lies in the enhancement of the core city as a market-place. This requires the making of downtown into an appealing and accessible area to industries, people and vehicles in order for it to achieve centripetal drawing power throughout an urban area. Downtown must be made attractive to industrial concentration, shoppers, commuters, and businessmen. This conception inevitably couples planning with urban renewal, area redevelopment, highways, streets, parking and mass transit.[37]

The fight against central city traffic congestion must be multifaceted to be effective. It should offer a full complement of services: (a) the replacement of open parking lots by multi-story parking garages; (b) the construction of multi-level highways, pedestrian podiums, causeways and arcades, and a suspended monorail. These will permit a vertical expansion of a city's traffic facilities; (c) a subterranean expansion for parking spaces by constructing underground garages; (d) on the ground level belt highways and limited-access throughways will relieve streets of all but local traffic. Concurrently, one-way streets, computer-synchronized traffic lights, special vehicular lanes and strictly enforced parking regulations, will aid in smoother and more efficient traffic flow; and, finally (e) the development of mass-transit facilities, aided by public subsidy.[38] A coordinated and synchronized transportation system, offering a versatile range of service and alternatives is the crux of a forward-looking transportation plan.[39]

[37] William L. Baldwin, "Economic Aspects of Business Blight and Traffic Congestion," *Taming Megalopolis,* Vol. I, *What Is and What Could Be,* H. Wentworth Eldredge (ed.) (Garden City, N.Y.: Anchor Books, Doubleday and Co., Inc., 1967).

[38] *Ibid.*

[39] John W. Dyckman, "Transportation in Cities," *Cities* (New York: Alfred A. Knopf, A Scientific American Book, 1969).

The dispersal effect of the automobile must be checked if "compact cities with centrally located places of work, relatively high-density residential zones, concentration of shopping and public facilities as well as employment,"[40] is the goal. The irony of anything less than massive transportation manipulation is that

> . . . additional accommodation creates additional traffic. The opening of a freeway designed to meet existing demand may eventually increase that demand until congestion on the freeway increases the travel time to what it was before the freeway existed.[41]

Also, in the case of the central city, unless it undergoes renovation, the addition of freeways, on balance, would improve centrifugal access and, ironically, add to decentralization.[42] There are also social costs to be measured against economic advantages. The construction of freeways causes displacement of residents and may add to pollution. Massive transportation reconstruction would entail massive displacements of this kind, but the balanced transportation system would, of course, minimize pollution. From past experience, it would appear that piecemeal treatments of the transportation problem "must be recognized as rather indirect attacks on the basic difficulties of poor land-use patterns, declining populations and tax bases, and unequal sharing of public burdens."[43] Yet, a massive approach to transportation facilitation requires a degree of metropolitan governmental cooperation and fiscal outlay rarely found.[44] The present transportation system has inclined toward facilitating spatial dispersal and, in effect, is crucial in the determination of the pattern of urban expansion and population location.

[40] *Ibid.*, p. 145.
[41] *Ibid.*
[42] Altschuler, *op. cit.*
[43] John R. Meyer, "Knocking Down the Straw Men," in Chinitz (ed.), *op. cit.*, p. 93.
[44] The Bay Area Rapid Transit System (BART) is a positive example of intergovernmental cooperation for the foundation of an effective public transport system.

Urban Renewal. Urban renewal is directly related to the quest for the revitalization of improved downtown land values, and the return of middle- and upper-income groups to the city. Urban renewal started out theoretically as a New Deal panacea for the welfare of the poor, by the way of improved housing and environment, through public rather than market forces.[45] Title I of the Housing Act of 1949 transformed redevelopment into a mechanism for stimulating the private housing market by defraying redevelopment costs through federal loans. Meanwhile, grants to cities covered the two-thirds difference between the city's purchase price of land and its sale price to private developers. Subsequent amendments to the Housing Act were designed to emphasize the rehabilitation and conservation of neighborhoods by guaranteeing Federal funds for this purpose (1954), and in 1956, provision of Federal funds for the relocation of the displaced. The amendments' reference to conservation and rehabilitation downgraded the until-then prevalently used bulldozer, and broadened the category of redevelopment areas to include parts of the city other than residential neighborhoods.[46] State enabling legislation also encourages redevelopment by providing legal mechanisms which permit local agencies to condemn private property, not only for public uses and for publicly-owned housing, but also for their resale to private developers who agreed to fulfill the agency's area plan.[47]

Urban renewal has now evolved into a seeming compromise between social reformers and economic maximizers by endeavoring to provide decent living conditions for slumdwellers while at the same time stimulating large-scale

[45] Nathan Glazer, "The Renewal of Cities." in *Cities, op. cit.*

[46] Jewel Bellush and Murray Hausknecht, "Urban Renewal: An Historical Overview," *Urban Renewal: People, Politics, and Planning,* Bellush and Hausknecht (eds.) (Garden City, N.Y.: Anchor Books, Doubleday & Co., 1967).

[47] This practice was upheld by the U.S. Supreme Court in *Berman* v. *Parker,* 348, U.S. 26 (1954), which ruled that eminent domain was lawful even if for private use if the area condemned was "injurious to the public health, safety, morals, and welfare of the inhabitants."

private rebuilding in the hope of revitalizing downtown areas, halting the exodus of middle-class whites, and gaining badly needed tax revenues.[48] While the compromise ideally appears a just conciliation of conflicting interests, practically they remain conflicting and contradictory.

> An urban renewal project is usually a partnership between governmental and private interests; the government procures the site, using its powers of condemnation as necessary, and it turns the site over to private redevelopers at a substantial discount from the acquisition price. The private redeveloper, therefore, must see a possibility for profit; he must see an opportunity to rebuild on the site and to find renters or buyers for the new properties.[49]

For redevelopment to effectively fulfill the city's goals of attracting private investment and recapturing the middle class, it must be accomplished in vast parcels—by square miles rather than piddling areas[50]—in order to insulate the redeveloped area from an encroaching slum. Redevelopment in small parcels enclosed by run-down neighborhoods holds little possibility for enhanced land values or attraction for investors and middle-class families.[51]

Detractors of redevelopment on the basis of social injustices see it as the squandering of billions of dollars of taxpayers money for private profit, the destruction of countless low-rent homes, the seizure of one man's property for another's gain, and the forcible displacement of slum dwellers in the pursuit of fiscal aggrandizement.[52] Despite the 1954 Housing Act's requirement that a locality in formulating a

---

[48] Herbert J. Gans, "The Failure of Urban Renewal: A Critique and Some Proposals," in Bellush and Hausknecht (eds.), *op. cit.,* p. 173.

[49] Ray Vernon, "The Myth and Reality of Our Urban Problems," in Bellush and Hausknecht (eds.), *op. cit.*

[50] *Ibid.*

[51] *Ibid.*

[52] Martin Anderson, "Consequences of Urban Renewal," *Urban America: Crisis and Opportunity,* Jim Chard and Jon York (eds.) (Belmont, Calif.: Dickenson Publishing Co., Inc., 1969).

"Workable Program for Community Improvement" include a feasible plan for the relocation of displaced families in order to receive urban renewal assistance, the plight of displaced slum-dwellers for new housing has been acute.[53] Slum-dwellers are blocked from the suburbs by land development controls and stringent building codes, and they are evicted from the cities to make way for middle-class-living development programs and highway construction.[54] Denied access to housing in surrounding areas because of race, displaced slum-dwellers relocate to public-housing projects[55] or crowd into unreconstructed slums.

As yet unresolved by urban renewal and slum-dweller relocation, such as it is, are economic opportunities for these low-skilled groups. Relocation leaves them no closer to industries in outlying areas that could utilize their labor. Still unfulfilled by renewal diluted by political compromise to small-parcel development, is the promise of economic improvement and the return of the middle-class. For redevelopment to be economically feasible and attractive, it must be done in substantial parcels. For relocation of displaced persons to result in improved living conditions, a whole set of revolutionary changes must take place. Anti-discrimination laws have done little to change existent population patterns in the short-run and the urban socio-economic crisis is immediate. The poor must be relocated in areas requiring unskilled labor. To do so in large numbers in view of the present disposition of suburbs which precludes the poor from their communities, will require the construction of new towns with Federal financial assistance to metropolitan (regional) areas.

[53] Robert Weaver, "The Urban Complex," in Bellush and Hausknecht (eds.), *op. cit.*

[54] Bernard J. Frieden, "Toward Equality of Urban Opportunity," in Eldredge (ed.), *op. cit.*

[55] Public housing projects meet with a great deal of community opprobrium, and their development requires a great deal of political finesse and skill. Martin Meyerson and Edward Banfield, *Politics, Planning, and the Public Interest, the Case of Public Housing in Chicago* (The Free Press of Glencoe, New York: Crowell-Collier Publishing Co., 1964).

Raymond Vernon has proposed that building codes be relaxed in these new towns to make $6,000 to $8,000 dwellings once more available.[56] This will enable the new residents to acquire property, with the aid of government guaranteed loans, and to be near industries which would provide them with gainful employment. It is, after all,

> . . . a little ironic to lock the poor into structures in the old city which are unhealthful and unsafe in the interests of protecting them from lesser risks in a much more healthful and safe setting.[57]

The relocation of the poor in improved housing conditions, a better environment, and proximity to economic opportunities, would also, then, allow redevelopment of blighted areas on a full-scale to the advantage of public and private interests. Then, and only then, can urban renewal be a compromise between the fulfillment of the housing needs of the poor and the fiscal and aesthetic needs of the city.

Zoning. The planning agency's daily business invariably includes some aspect of zoning. Zoning, a technique which began in the 1920's as a device to insulate the single-family district and property values from "encroachments," remains unchanged, if however, more sophisticated.[58] Its original trilogy of hard-set classifications of residential, commercial, and industrial zones has since become more flexible. Although the overriding concerns in suburbia are more social than economic, communities nonetheless are eager to gain "fashionable" industries such as light industry and research centers that are popularly believed to add more to tax revenues than

[56] It may also be necesary to encourage such innovative techniques in building construction as to minimize labor costs and capital outlay. However, this would involve the monumental task of overcoming the resistance of entrenched craft-unions with their vested interest in maintaining the status-quo in construction practices.

[57] Raymond Vernon, "The Myth and Reality of Our Urban Problems," in Chinitz (ed.), *op. cit.*

[58] Babcock, *The Zoning Game, op. cit.*

they require in municipal services.[59] Thus, zoning is attuned to economic realities and can adjust to fit existing circumstances.

Flexibility in zoning is achieved through discretionary practices suited to specific circumstance. These include zoning variances, "floating" zones, and "contract" zones. Zoning variances—an *ad hoc,* discretionary permit—may be granted as relief from "unnecessary hardship." "Floating" zones, although mentioned in the text of an ordinance, are not found on a map and allow local government a great deal of discretion. Most discretionary, "contract" zones are covenants or easements granted by a sitting legislature and subject to negotiation between a municipality and a prospective developer.[60] While these methods of zoning are in consideration of economic impacts upon land-use policy, the *sine qua non* of suburban zoning is to maintain market values, residential purity and low density in medium and high-cost subdivisions, for socially homogeneous communities.[61]

Rational theory holds that zoning is needed for the maintenance of property values and for the operational requirements of planning.[62] The sanctity of property values apparently has necessitated the exclusion of anyone or anything that threatens their maintenance. The planning exigency suggests zoning as a means of insuring the rationality of a community comprehensive plan by facilitating the acquisition of data and general surveys, and by officially delineating a proposed plan of development. Hence, zoning is the integral link between physical arrangements and property values, with a community's plan calling for property value zoning, and property value zoning shaping the plan.

"Zoning," in effect, "has been a positive force shaping the character of the municipality to fit its frequently vague but nevertheless powerful preconceptions."[63]

[59] *Ibid.*
[60] *Ibid.*
[61] *Ibid.*
[62] *Ibid.*
[63] *Ibid.,* p. 122.

The Post-Industrial City

We have moved fitfully into the post-industrial city, and the city of set boundaries, static populations, and economic and social *autarkie* has passed away. It has, instead, become the metropolis—the urban metropolitan area—perhaps in transition to megalopolis or even ecumenopolis. Yet, municipal government is not attuned to this passage of time, and continues to do "business-as-usual" with unfettered nonchalance. Municipal government and planning, which is a part of it, have reached a historic crossroad, a point similarly and dramatically reached by economics four decades ago when the irrelevance of classical economics was exposed. Although our economic system adapted to contemporary realities, our local governmental system remains unmoved while the city bursts beyond control.

The cluster of people, businesses, and interactions within a spatially confined area has been transformed into a spatially dispersed yet high-density cluster of people, businesses, and interactions spilling beyond municipal boundaries and governmental jurisdictions. This is the metropolitan region of a great deal of economic, social and personal interdependence. A municipality, interacting with neighboring municipalities, is as much dependent upon its neighbor as upon itself for its development. Whatever occurs in this sprawling agglomeration affects everything within it.

Along with every other metropolitan aspect, governmental interdependence is "a fact of life";[64] and planning cannot stop at the city boundary. The heavily private ethos and parochialism of autonomous municipalities is unresponsive to pressing public needs. The divergencies and self-seeking of independent localities have created a sense of political anarchy in the urban environment.

Comprehensive planning is self-defeative when it is restricted to a defined locality. Though charged with formulat-

[64] Graham S. Finney, "The Intergovernmental Context of Local Planning," in Goodman and Freund (eds.), *op. cit.*

ing long-run development it is handicapped in fulfilling rational design by the imposition of unrealistic parameters. Any action conforming to a dubious comprehensive plan is, at best, palliative. Urban renewal and transportation policies implemented for the sake of securing the economic advantage, or alleviating the fiscal disadvantage, of one municipality over another is promulgating competition and localism among interdependent neighbors. It is the shortsighted perpetuation of a Hobbesian state of nature, a "war of all against all."

The larger cities are tending to become concentration points of low income groups and require disproportionately large outlays for welfare and social development. Many cities are increasingly impressed with the necessity for large-scale rehabilitation and redevelopment if they are to compete with the suburbs as places to live and do business, and if they are to avoid untimely obsolescence of private and public investment in their central areas. In the suburbs, rapid expansion requires enormous amounts of new capital facilities in the form of streets, schools, recreational facilities, and the like.

The advent of the metropolitan age and the concomitant development of modern urban culture are creating new demands for many government services and increasing standards of other services. Many of the emergent needs can be supplied only by new governmental agencies designed to operate on a metropolitan scale.[65]

Systems Planning

Systems planning transforms the amorphous agglomerations, that are typical of urban areas, into cohesive, unified, organic wholes. But systems planning is only a technique, albeit the most rational one, for acquiring a comprehensive awareness of interactions and interfunctional effects upon the system under scrutiny. Planning agencies, utilizing the unifying principle of systems-analysis, are producing technically correct plans that influence the regulation and direction of urban development. But the obstructionism of political lo-

[65] Lyle C. Fitch, "Metropolitan Financial Problems," in Chinitz (ed.), *op. cit.*, p. 114.

calism and governmental fragmentation obviate the implementation of relevant area-wide plans.

If we are to create life-enhancing surroundings in both
cities and suburbs, the first requirement is the power to
plan and to implement programs which encompass the
total problems of metropolitan regions. Air and water
pollution, recreation, and provision for adequate mass
transit are region-wide problems, but in most areas action
is hampered by legal impediments which actually prevent
regional planning. As long as each city, county, township,
and district can obstruct or curtail, planning for the future
cannot be effective. The cities and metropolitan areas that
are devising new political institutions for regional planning
are today's pioneers of urban conservation.[66]

Urban systems planning is total planning for an inclusive
metropolitan area or region. It takes into consideration the
entire urban system of interdependencies and the public need.
In juxtaposition, contemporary local community planning,
hampered by a tortuous political decision-making process, is
limited planning within the restrictions of a client's ethos. To
dramatize the inadequacy of restricted and spasmodic planning, typical of many communities, is the example of zoning
practices or urban redevelopment without consideration to
the intricate web of interdependencies.

It is impossible to conceive of good housing down-
wind from a factory spewing ashes and noxious gases, in
neighborhoods so poorly served by local government that
trash and filth dominate the scene, in sections where open
sewers or seepage from septic tanks spread disease, or
adjacent to rivers or ponds that would poison or infect anyone who used the water for swimming.[67]

If planning is to become an instrument for defining a
whole range of needs connected with urban life, it must

[66] Stuart L. Udall, *The Quiet Crisis* (New York: Holt, Rinehart
and Winston, 1963), p. 165.

[67] U.S., Congress, House, *Building the American City,* Report of
the National Commission on Urban Problems to the Congress and to
the President of the United States, 91st Cong., 1st Sess., December 12,
1968, House Doc. No. 91–34.

attain its perspective from the available range of interrelationships. The realization that a set of public policy variables exerts influence on patterns of urban development intensifies the requirement for a regionally coordinated approach to transportation, tax policies, water and sewerage systems, air pollution control, and so on.[68] Coordination in policy formulation affords consideration to social costs as well as the realization of sounder fiscal results and a rational pattern of development.

If the interest is to exercise some consistent and raional guidance over urban expansion, logic will surely argue for some form of coordinated public works programming in an intergovernmental framework for joint action.[69]

[68] Chapin, F. Stuart, Jr., in Eldredge (ed.), Vol. II, *op. cit.*
[69] *Ibid.,* p. 739.

VI

Planning for the
Urban Nation

The concept of the city as a physical artifact is being replaced by one in which interaction and relation are emphasized. The new city may be identified as a density configuration that is measured by the flows of interaction within a given "matrix." This matrix, however, has no firm boundaries but represents a continuum of densities of interaction where the actual lines of division become more or less arbitrary symbols just down for convenience. The metropolitan region is the new, etherealized city.[1]

American city governments exert control over the physical disposition of activities by means of zoning regulations, tax and assessment tactics, capital investment decisions, subdivision controls over vacant land, urban renewal and public housing programs, and building and occupancy codes. City

[1] John Friedmann, "Regional Planning as a Field of Study," *Regional Development and Planning, A Reader,* John Friedmann and William Alonso, (eds.) (Cambridge, Mass.: The Massachusetts Institute of Technology Press, 1964), p. 66.

planning, as a device of city governments, is concerned mainly with the creation of a more efficient spatial environment within the purview of governmental influence and laws. It is, therefore, an activity which seeks the stimulation of public services and market decisions to effect a desired spatial pattern in a microenvironment. However,

> . . . [decisions] in this sphere of planning may have implications at the regional and even the national level. Renewal and housing policies that call for reductions of central city density, for example, will exert powerful influences in shaping the settlement pattern of the metropolitan area, since the overspill of population will usually locate elsewhere in the larger community.[2]

Regional planning pertains to the process of the ordering of human activities in supra-urban space through a spatial perspective of resource allocations and economic development. "Regional policy should be thought of as a tool for comprehensive national development in which all parts of the country contribute in their own ways to the attainment of national objectives."[3] However, planning, whether it be in intra-urban or supra-urban space, operates within a political matrix and, thus, must be formulated with reference to the spatial structure of political authority and decisions. City planning confines itself to the city as its spatial unit, but regional planning, by definition, is concerned with larger spatial units and, therefore, focuses on the first spatially organized level which is greater than the city—the metropolitan region.

Although city and regional planning approaches synthesize in the metropolitan region with their common interest in spatial organization, there are distinct differences between the two approaches, other than the obvious distinction of scale. Fundamental to their differentiation are the disparate institutional settings for public policy execution which affect the functional perception and performance of the respective planning orientations. Regional planning concerns the spatial

---

[2] *Ibid.,* pp. 67–68.
[3] *Ibid.,* p. 65.

structuring of economic development, with activity and physical patterns as interrelated expressions of the same reality. Activity patterns are the flows of commodities, labor and capital, and communications which form a confluence with physical components—human settlements, transportation networks, and the like—in space. Hence, whereas city planning is confined to physical land use and design in the organization of space, and the preparation of investment schemes for its actualization, regional planning is charged with the influencing of the development process itself.

The task of regional planning is the formulation of regional development strategies for the allocation of resources in space, the location of productive facilities, and the organization of settlement patterns.

The linking of critical control centers that perform planning functions in various urban regions permits strategies on an interregional as well as intraregional dimension. Broader strategic considerations are afforded by the identification of the patterns of functional interconnections of the metropolitan regions to a larger spatial framework. This enables a multidimensional perspective of the implications of the spatial arrangements of resources and activities. A multi-dimensional framework of critical control centers can allow a rational comprehensive development strategy at the national policy level; it can provide for orderly settlement and economic patterns at the regional level, and integrate that level into the national space economy, and finally, at the local level, regional and city planning skills can meet and merge to focus on the myriad problems of a growing metropolis.

The concept of regional planning's superspace—which in addition to the three dimensions of geometric space, and time, includes as many other dimensions as there are states of interaction and interdependence—is illusory.

It would require the discovery and definition of the fundamental variables and their organization into a taxonomy which classified them into discrete, nonoverlapping elements. Yet the very concept of such a superspace makes clear that any partial space is a selective simplification, implying a purpose in including some things and excluding others. When that purpose is a cognitive one, the space will include those elements necessary to explain or describe the phenomena that interest us. When the purpose is normative, the space must be formulated with a view to the effectiveness of action upon it. Thus the very definition of region will vary with our purpose. A region defined for water control will be very different from one for the integration of the iron and steel industry or from one for the measurement of the multipler effects of an investment. For some purposes our region may be an area, while for others, such as urban renewal, it may consist of points which are not joined. In short, the nature of the space in any case will depend both on the type of interrelationships being considered and on the purpose in mind.[4]

Operating in a dynamic space of ever-wider and more complex interrelations, the regional planning process is the merger of functional and physical planning in order to influence these interrelationships. Unable to conceptualize ideal spatial boundaries for planning, it must nonetheless compromise and adopt one, to be functionally operative. A region may, thus, be founded on "a certain regularity and order in the structure of space as it is shaped by human activities."[5] These structures can be perceived as a system of settlement nodes and their functional linkages. The nodes are within a physically dispersed loose hierarchical framework which is internally differentiated by function, and each node is characterized by a "density field" of functional interactions with a decline in interaction with increasing removedness from the center. The loosely structured nodes are themselves located within a functional interaction gravitational field of a nodal center, with a decrease in interrelated attraction as distance from the center increases, until activity interactions are no longer coincident. Hence, in effect, the basic unit for regional

[4] John Friedmann and William Alonso, "Space and Planning," in *Regional Development and Planning, A Reader, op. cit.*

[5] Friedmann, "Regional Planning as a Field of Study," *op. cit.*, p. 62.

planning has described the metropolitan region. It is at this level that critical control centers are founded and the linking of these control centers in supra-urban space creates the framework for strategic planning.

Planning for the Metropolis

Metropolitan planning is the intricate coordination of action by local and state governments, and federal agencies, and the adjustment of these policies to the vagaries of market forces, for the realization of effective guidance of metropolitan development. It plays a central role in conflicts of interest resolution by contributing to the arbitration of conflicts through posing the issues and alternative courses of action in an analytical framework. Metropolitan planning can, through its expertise, overcome the narrow parochialism of local units by reconciling these entities to coordinated and cooperative activities on behalf of mutual advantages, such as the broad gains of economic growth within a region. Metropolitan planning is the link between the municipalities and the federal system, in that it speaks for area-wide interests to the upper echelons of government, and, by the same token, is the conduit for a coherent intergovernmental output of policies affecting its area of influence.

Metropolitan planning activities benefit governmental units and agencies, market interests, and citizens of the metropolitan area.[6] It provides local jurisdictions with technical assistance, rational decision making on the basis of metropolitan studies and projections, and the opportunity to join in determinations concerning both the region and the local community. It can augment the legislative and administrative abilities of the states, as well as those of the localities, once planning staffs achieve the necessary body of technical studies and projections.

[6] U.S., Congress, Senate, Subcommittee on Intergovernmental Relations of the Committee on Government Operations, in Cooperation with the Joint Center for Urban Studies of the Massachusetts Institute of Technology and Harvard University, *The Effectiveness of Metropolitan Planning* (Washington, D.C.: June 30, 1964).

Metropolitan planning agencies can serve as staff extensions of State executive agencies and of the State legislature, giving advice on the probable effects upon metropolitan development of such State measures as highway construction, park acquisition, housing programs, and tax policies involving local governments. This type of technical advice is particularly important for the implementation of State policies concerning economic development, education, recreation, transportation, and housing— for such policies must be worked out to an increasing extent within the States' urban areas.[7]

In addition to influencing state and local decision-making through providing improved information, regional planning can also abate the conflict between state and local perspectives regarding metropolitan development. Metropolitan planning agencies can be of service to the heavily involved federal government by acting as a clearinghouse in forging greater areal coordination of federal programs.

The contributions of metropolitan planning to metropolitan development may be perceived in terms of its functions as an intergovernmental liaison, policy adviser, and educator of the general public. The first would involve taking the initiative in bringing governments and public agencies together for a coordinated impact on mutually acceptable objectives. Secondly, regional planning provides advice to the public decision making process by presenting cogent studies and informed alternatives which would suggest feasible and practicable approaches to short- and long-run problem-solving. Private capital may also avail itself of this information in order to make rational considerations of current and future investments. Finally, planning can enlist the interest and participation of private citizens by enlightening them about metropolitan problems and affording them opportunities for choices about their environment's development.

With the notion of coalescing the fragmented local political units into larger areal units inhibited by the realities of the American political culture and the irrelevance of coin-

---

[7] *Ibid.*, p. 11.

ciding political space with physical and activity space, metropolitan planning becomes the feasible device for functionally integrating the disparate, yet interrelated units. It is just as efficient as functional special districts, and, in addition, offers the advantages of political responsibility and responsiveness. This is accomplished by assuring the participation of local units in decisions which affect their constituents, and this is especially visible when the planning process is institutionally incorporated within councils of government. There are also, with positive as well as negative implications, exploitable fissures in the planning activity:

> Decision-makers in regional planning units, made responsible to a large and independent constituency by the process of approval of the area plan, are forced to consider a multiplicity of cross pressures from elected officials, local planners, authority members, and private property owners.[8]

While this is exemplary from the standpoint of achieving democratic consensus by providing a forum for information and debate and finally, a negotiated compromise settlement, it is as well, the reiteration of "free market" liberalism at the expense of rational decision-making. It would seem logical that in the course of the plan's development, planners must be absolved of vested influences, so that the plan may be a reflection of the most informed inputs, in order to present the political decision-makers with the soundest available alternatives. The decisive implementation of the plan is subjected to myriad pressures, and rightly so. Practically, however, planners must at all times be sensitized to their social and political environment, or else, in a democratic society, become meaningless and impotent bureaucrats. If planning is to fulfill its vital function as a countervailing and coordinating device among government levels it must adapt to a political system of conflict and diversity of interest.

For planning to be an effective tool for metropolitan development under the circumstances, it must effect methods

---

[8] *Ibid.*, pp. 27–28.

of conflict resolution. Generally, there are three effective routines for peacefully resolving conflicts:

(1) by the existence or exercise of an authority strong enough to coerce others into a solution

(2) by the existence of the psychological feeling of identification

(3) by the workings of a negotiating process in which one party tries to convince the other that the latter's best chance of maximizing his returns is to accept a particular solution.[9]

The authority structure in metropolitan areas does not resemble Hobbes' model in "The Leviathan" of a focus of power preponderant over all rival factions. Instead, the political framework is characterized by decisions emanating from the interactions among coexisting power centers, as an ideal of John C. Calhoun's "concurrent majorities" with power for resolution lying in "the momentum created by differentiated forces which for diverse reasons seek to prevent action."[10] Hence, the planning agency's role in conflict resolution is often constituted by forces external to the metropolitan political arena. This intends the authority vested in the agency to review and comment on the effect a state or federally financed local project may have on the area-wide plan for the metropolitan area; and with these comments commanding the attention of the state and federal disbursing agencies. This is a more positive role for the planning agency than has been designed in programs which provide solely for recommendations to the local jurisdictions which retain the option for their acceptance or rejection. Thus, the authority bases of metropolitan planning agencies are derived from the state and federal levels which seek to maximize the effect of their fiscal expenditures by the most efficient management of metropolitan issues. Additional support can be expected from the units—functional or political—which would obtain advantages from the programs endorsed by the planning agency.

[9] *Ibid.*, p. 32.
[10] *Ibid.*

The role of metropolitan planning is politically handicapped by the absence of a public identity with the metropolitan area. Consequently, the nonexistence of a metropolitan community of individuals sharing values and identifying with the aggregate has dispelled the legitimacy of metropolitan planning as a decision making unit. The lack of community identification has at best, caused a lack of citizens' participation in area-wide affairs, and at worst, psychologically defined metropolitan planning as a threat to the interests of existing jurisdictions.

However, the existence of a metropolitan planning agency may be self-reinforcing in creating community identification. The agency's functional performance in promoting solutions to common problems may lessen the gap between public expectations and government action, and provide the public with a visible entity appropriate for acting on its demands. Thus,

> . . . while the metropolitan area is not now a psychological community, it is a spatially-defined unit with functional significance reflecting the interdependence of its inhabitants. Experience indicates that as geographical space becomes more consciously recognized as a social fact, here through the work of the agency making the metropolitan area a site for social interaction, the sense of community will increase.[11]

Negotiation is generally acknowledged as the most fruitful device for conflict resolution. But,

> . . . [in] the past, it is hardly surprising that bargaining, in the absence of an authority with the interests of the metropolitan area in mind, has proved incapable of producing the kind of long-range program needed to direct area development. Without an agency committed to regional goals, what occurs is competitive bargaining among muncipalities, interested only in serving their residents, and public corporations, committed by statute to concern themselves with specific functional fields. This decentral-

[11] *Ibid.*

ization is incompatible with the production and implementation of comprehensive plans to guide growth in the
future.[12]

Despite the presence of an area-wide planning agency,
bargaining is the framework in which the process of developing and implementing a plan unavoidably occurs. In this
environment, the implementation of regional plans can be
aided by legal standards enhancing the authority of the
planning agency, and the development of the legitimizing
identification mechanism. At any rate, planning can aid the
bargaining process on behalf of more rational development
by awakening an awareness of the communality of goals.
This is done by persuasive demonstration of the areas where
local interests coincide and the advantages inherent in cooperation. Additionally, planning's research ability and the
concomitant presentation of incisive alternatives for efficacious decision-making augment the reconciliation of diversity
in favor of a broadened perspective under the auspices of the
planning agency's expertise. The bargaining situation can,
thus, be equated

> . . . to the situation in business called mutual inter-
> dependence, recognized in oligopolistic competition. There
> each firm is aware that an apparently beneficial short-term
> action, like a price cut, will lead to a future response by
> others nullifying the original act. Then all prices will fall
> and the only result will be that all firms suffer in the long
> run. On the metropolitan scene we must enable the plan-
> ning agency to be the intelligence mechanism; with its eye
> on the long-run gains it must have the power to show
> participants where making short-run sacrifices will result
> in greater future benefits.[13]

The contributions of metropolitan planning agencies
may range from establishing strategic controls influencing
regional development to mundane activities regarding non-
controversial matters. The latter formulations would involve

[12] *Ibid.*, p. 35.
[13] *Ibid.*, p. 37.

some of the basic techniques of city planning such as the identification of physical locations suitable for delineated functions, and the preparation of studies dealing with problems of traffic congestion, mass transportation, urban renewal, and the like. The former would entail more elaborate studies of sensitive issues, and a prescient manipulation of public and private policies to a desired environmental arrangement of activities and places.

The technical activities of a regional planning agency are structured according to a hierarchy of complexity. The simplest level of technical activity is the accumulation of a data inventory of the metropolitan area; the next level of complexity would invoke analyses and forecasts for the determination of trends in metropolitan development; and the most elaborate technical operation would include the preparation of a comprehensive metropolitan plan.

The provision of a data inventory, albeit recognized as a minimal effort toward regional coherence, is an effective process for conflict resolution. The assembling of a mosaic of individual plans enables the area-wide agency to identify the inconsistencies between the projects of various differentiated communities. Thus, calling attention to such incongruities as a proposed housing project in one community across the boundary from a planned garbage dump in a contiguous community, or an urban renewal endeavor proposed in the path of a new state freeway, is a crucial service to the fragmented political system.

The more complex task of metropolitan analyses and projections requires a larger technical staff versed in the aspects of city and regional planning. The focus of their activities would be on the forecast of future conditions—in housing, transportation demand, private investment, general pattern of land use, and so on—the probable development course, and a projection of the development's distribution within the region under study. The forecast of growth and development patterns is a studied prediction of expected, fundamental demands upon the region's resources. This analysis provides the background for informed local, state, and federal decisions about the metropolis, and may serve as a reservoir of regional data that public and private decision makers can utilize.

The probable effect of this additional information will be sounder and less wasteful decisions about new investments in the region's physical facilities and services, and a wiser use of both public and private resources within the region. Also, more accurate information as to future conditions may serve to stimulate private investment within the area.[14]

The preparation of a comprehensive area-wide plan involves the functional integration of the data inventory and the analyses and forecasts into a presentation of alternative modes for future development. The suggestion of alternatives would depict varying patterns of growth under various sets of policies, and offer an evaluation of the different modes. Intrinsic to the alternatives for growth and development would be the criteria of a strategy for controls and policies necessary for influencing the patterns of activity and settlement. The selection of control devices determines the preference for activities which would induce such aspects of development as character and location of industrial and employment centers, types of transportation systems, and concentrated or dispersed physical patterns. The choice of alternative and the implementing decision is done by political actors, but the planning agency retains the responsibility for overseeing the development's adherence to the plan, and adjusts the strategy to a compatibility with environmental realities.

Finally, the existence of area-wide planning mechanisms does not preclude the persistence of local planning. In fact, it is the coexistence of regional plans and the many local plans which energizes the vital role of area-wide coordinator of the regional planning bodies. It is the collaboration of the local and regional plans which consummates a coherent articulation of the metropolitan area's needs by skillful and

[14] *Ibid.*, p. 23.

coordinated applications within the micro- and macro-environments. The macro-space orientation of regional planning is aided in its holistic approach by the inputs of local data and idiosyncracies which the micro-focus of planning's sub-units can offer. Conversely, the comprehensive view of the regional entity is indispensible for the rational development of the urban area.

Profile of Metropolitan Planning Agencies[15]

Comprehensive metropolitan planning is a post-World War II phenomenon although a few earlier examples of comprehensive planning had occurred. The best known early plan is "The Regional Plan for New York and Its Environs" completed in 1929.

Although public planning commissions are founded under provisions of a state enabling act, the recent growth of area-wide planning agencies is connected with federal acts conditioning grants-in-aid for local projects upon advance review and comment of a metropolitan planning unit. The federal stimulus is based on the concept that planning is the most feasible method of executing coordinated development of metropolitan areas. Fundamental to the notion of planning's potential efficacy for providing a coherence to area-wide

[15] "1968 Survey of Metropolitan Planning," Graduate School of Public Affairs, State University of New York at Albany; Joseph F. Zimmerman (ed.), *Government of the Metropolis, Selected Readings* (New York: Holt, Rinehart and Winston, Inc., 1968); John Friedmann, "The Concept of a Planning Region—the Evolution of an Idea in the United States," in Friedman and Alonso (eds.), *op. cit.;* U.S., Congress, House, A Study Submitted to the Intergovernmental Relations Subcommittee of the Committee on Government Operations by the Advisory Committee on Intergovernmental Relations, *Metropolitan America: Challenge to Federalism* (Washington, D.C.: U.S. Government Printing Office, October, 1966); Advisory Commission on Intergovernmental Relations, *Urban America and the Federal System, Commission Findings and Proposals,* M-47 (Washington, D.C.: October, 1969); Joseph F. Zimmerman (ed.), *1968 Metropolitan Area Annual* (Albany, N.Y.: Graduate School of Public Affairs, State University of New York at Albany, 1968); *The Effectiveness of Metropolitan Planning, op. cit.*

matters, however, is the conclusion that metropolitan planning can only be effective insofar as there is collaboration between the decision makers and the planners. Accordingly, this led to federal legislation endorsing the involvement of the decision makers in the planning process and requiring that area-wide reviews of local applications be made by a metropolitan planning agency under the auspices of a council of cooperating local jurisdictions.

The Housing and Urban Development Act of 1965, which amended the Housing Act of 1954, was the legislation expressly enacted to energize the development of organizations of local elected officials in metropolitan areas and to encourage their involvement in comprehensive planning. This was done by making the councils eligible to receive federal financial aid for the preparation of comprehensive metropolitan plans, so long as the councils were composed primarily of elected municipal and county officials. The upsurge in metropolitan planning activities and growth of councils of government can be attributed primarily to this landmark legislation. Subsequent federal legislation[16] and administrative policy[17] were to further stimulate the development of metropolitan planning by making these agencies "review-and-comment" clearinghouses for all federal aid for urban projects. The interest of the federal government in the resolution of metropolitan problems can be discerned in the extent of financial commitments—primarily through conditional grants-in-aid to state and local governments—which increased from $894 million in 1946 to an estimated $30 billion in fiscal year 1971 of which approximately $18.7 billion was lavished upon the Standard Metropolitan Statistical Areas (SMSA).

The profile of the average metropolitan planning agency is a composite of size, areal jurisdiction, finances, and func-

[16] Demonstration Cities and Metropolitan Development Act of 1966, Public Law 89–754.

[17] U.S., Bureau of the Budget, "Circular No. A-82," April 11, 1967; U.S., Bureau of the Budget, "Areawide Agencies and Metropolitan Areas Designated under Sec. 104 of the Demonstration Cities and Metropolitan Development Act."

tions.[18] The average number of members serving on a metropolitan planning commission is 15.3. A majority of metropolitan planning bodies have territorial jurisdictions coterminous with their SMSA's, with the remainder's jurisdiction either greater or less than their SMSA's. The most common method for determining territorial jurisdiction is the use of county boundaries. Other techniques for areal allocations are agreements among the members, and state law. Revision of boundaries or dissolution of the commissions are commonly done by amendment of a joint powers agreement, and amendment of state law. The number of personnel—full-time and part-time professionals and non-professionals—employed on the staffs of metropolitan planning varies significantly, but a majority employ less than ten employees in each category.

Total operating budgets of metropolitan planning commissions have registered marked increases since 1963. The average operating budget per commission—$360,310—has increased 264 percent since 1963. Average state financial support has declined from $115,764 in 1963 to $31,969 in 1968; county support has also diminished. In contrast, municipalities have increased their financial contributions from an average of $31,543 in 1963 to appropriations of $56,375 in 1968. Expenditures have risen sharply from an average of $104,600 per commission in 1963 to $189,760 in 1968, an increase of 44.9 percent. Disbursements for staff services constitute the largest portion of total expenditures. A substantial share of the budgets is devoted to long-range planning; however, most commissions expend only a modest fraction for the services of consultants.

The planning program concentrates on general planning studies, with land use plans the most frequently undertaken task, followed by the preparation of transportation plans, water resources and air pollution abatement programs, and examination of community facilities and recreation. Although the average agency is authorized by state enabling legislation to prepare a comprehensive plan, the statutes do not require

[18] Profile based on 1968 data unless otherwise specified.

the local jurisdictions to adopt the plan. Additionally, designated agencies review and comment on local, state, or federally inspired projects within their jurisdiction, but their
determinations are left to the discretion of the submitting
body.

In 1972 there were 211 metropolitan area-wide agencies
specified to manage the review and comment task with respect
to 267 SMSA's.[19] Most of the federally designated agencies
have jurisdiction over entire SMSA's; some of them are assigned lesser areas than their SMSA's, but a number of the
agencies are tasked with a broader area, including the responsibility for two or more SMSA's. Review bodies may be single
county or city-county agencies, or regional planning commissions concerned with two or more counties. Some are voluntary
councils of government while the remainder are metropolitan
transportation or state planning agencies.

The common weaknesses of area-wide planning bodies
are the limited public support for metropolitan planning, uncertain and insufficient power, and inadequate staffs, and fiscal
revenues. Metropolitan planning may be in an inchoate stage
of regional coherence, but there is scant evidence to support
this. The regional planning function has been centered on
transposing local physical projects to a broader scale, albeit
its intent has been the consideration of activity interactions and
the devising of appropriate controls over these flows toward
the effectuation of a preferred development pattern. It has
been powerless to effect strategic planning on a regional level;
it has as yet, been unable to transcend the political existentialism of local jurisdictions, and to realize a sense of metropolitan
community. Its authority base is essentially derived from
sources external to the metropolitan environment in that it
is in its capacity as a federally designated review clearinghouse
that planning has had its most vital impact on rational urban
development.

A serious constraint to planning's efficacy is that it is

[19] Letter from Advisory Commission on Intergovernmental Relations, Washington, D.C.: March 8, 1972.

often considered by local authorities as an ethereal endeavor. These jurisdictions have seldom initiated a comprehensive planning function on the merits of its potential as an area-wide device for problem-solving, but rather have formed these agencies as a way of foreclosing an anticipated imposition of an integrating device from higher levels of government. Local units, too, have eagerly responded to the proffered federal, and to some extent, state grants which have induced the mushrooming of voluntary councils of government and regional planning bodies. However, the history of involving these area-wide mechanisms in mundane activities persuades a suspicion of the probity of the localities' intentions. Yet, there has been an increasing appreciation by the municipalities for some of the basic services that an area-wide mechanism performs, although they have been inhibited in allowing an exercise of its full potential. The past role of the states in support of the metropolitan agencies has been disappointing. The general experience of many area-wide planning bodies mocks the veracity of local intergovernmental cooperation and coordination, and exposes the condition of continued anarchy despite the well intentioned strategies at the federal level. The record of regional planning has prompted this description by John Friedmann: "This multiplicity of 'planning' is truly amazing; and yet there is no plan! A plan is largely an instrument for the integration and coordination of policies."[20]

Three Regional Institutions

The regional planning function is performed by a variety of structures. Currently the most fashionable governmental unit for this purpose, is the council of government. The Southern California Association of Governments (SCAG) is illustrative of the cooperative model for regional problem-solving and, hence, paradigmatic of the structural-functional characteristics of councils of governments. However, the cooperative models' less than dramatic results for regional

[20] John Friedmann, "The Concept of a Planning Region—The Evolution of an Idea in the United States," in Friedmann and Alonso (eds.), *op. cit.*, p. 499.

integration necessitates the evaluation of more forceful, if somewhat unique, paradigms. The Metropolitan Council of the Twin Cities Area, paradigmatic of intra-regional functional coordination, is indicative of a more compelling device. Most dynamic is the New York State Urban Development Corporation with its manifest and latent powers affording a vigorous state-level approach to ordered regional growth and development.

Cooperative Model: Southern California Association of Governments.

The Southern California Association of Governments is an agency voluntarily established by its member cities and counties persuant to the State of California Joint Exercise of Powers Act for the purpose of providing a forum for discussion, study, and development of recommendations on regional problems of mutual interest and concern regarding the orderly development of the Southern California region.[21]

On December 31, 1968, all six eligible counties—Imperial, Los Angeles, Orange, San Bernardino, Riverside and Ventura—and 97 out of 145 eligible cities were members; as of March 11, 1971, 110 cities have joined. The SCAG region consists of 38,641 square miles or 10.91 percent of the United States total of 3,541,072 square miles and 24.68 percent of the California total of 156,537 square miles.[22] The region's population, is over 10 million, more than 50 percent of California's population, and includes the city of Los Angeles with its population of approximately 2,800,000. In effect, the population of the SCAG region is greater than that of 46 states.

The Association's organizational structure is composed of a General Assembly, an Executive Committee, Policy and Technical Committees, and a professional staff. The General Assembly, consisting of one delegate and one alternate from

21 "Southern California Association of Governments, A Voluntary Advisory Forum of Cities and Counties," *SCAG,* February, 1969.

22 U.S., Department of Commerce, "County and City Data Book, 1967," Washington, D.C.

each member city and county and three delegates and three alternates from the City of Los Angeles, is the policy making aggregate of the Association. It convenes semi-annually in Spring and in the Fall. The Executive Committee, with a membership of 18 delegates and 18 alternates[23] from the General Assembly meets monthly and addresses itself to the substantive issues of the Association.[24] It is aided in its deliberations by the staff work and research of professional Association employees. Contributory to the affairs of the Association, and subsidiary to the General Assembly and Executive Committee, are the Policy and Technical Committees. Policy Committees are composed of elected local officials, appointed by the president of the Association, with an interest and expertise in a specific area of concern. Technical Committees are made up of highly skilled technical and administrative personnel in local government who advise the Policy Committees in pertinent substantive areas.

Policy Committees have been established for such functional areas as air pollution control, regional planning, information systems, transportation, water and waste management, aviation and airports, and parks and recreation. Technical Committees have been functionally structured as councils of air pollution control officers, airport administrators, park and recreation administrators, planners, engineers, and information systems analysts. Additionally, supplementing the formal policy and technical groups are two *ad hoc* committees established for consideration of developing programs in the field of citizen participation and regional comprehensive planning.

The explicit purpose of the Association and its continuing programs can be summarized as follows:

[23] An alternate may serve as a voting member in the absence of the officially appointed representative.

[24] In 1970 SCAG's Bylaws were amended to enlarge the Executive Committee from fifteen to eighteen members. This was done in order to allow for three At-Large delegates who would serve a one-year term. Santa Ana, Long Beach, and Compton were the cities selected for the At-Large posts. In 1971 each of these cities selected as either the delegate or the alternate to the Executive Committee a representative with a minority background.

Assemble, exchange, coordinate, and disseminate planning information on a region-wide basis to assist local government decision making and promote inter-governmental cooperation; Formulate positive recommendations of an advisory nature and encourage the development of a comprehensive planning process within the region; Participate with members and associated governments and citizen organizations in developing regional goals and stimulating discussion of regional problems; Provide a means of expression for local government points of view, and; Consider questions of mutual interest and concern to members in the field of creating governmental regional agencies.[25]

To finance its operations, the Association is supported by members' dues assessed one-half to the cities, one-half to the counties, and by federal government grants. As of December 1968, SCAG was the recipient of federal funding or approval of six grants totaling $915,012. This sum was supplemented by a mandatory local one-third matching contribution in cash or services, raising the total projects' cost to $1,372,517. "The grants cover overlapping periods, not necessarily calendar years, and it is difficult to give precise yearly budget figures for each grant."[26]

In keeping with its intent as a "voluntary advisory forum of cities and counties," SCAG's basic programs reflect a research and advisory bias, with preliminary steps undertaken in the regional planning effort. Its effectiveness in region-wide planning coordination was provided by its designation by the Bureau of the Budget as the area-wide "review and comment" agency. This review over federal grants for regional planning and development has energized the Association's commitment to intergovernmental coordination of plans and programs.

SCAG's principal functional programs concern the coordination of planning; coordination of development; infor-

[25] "Southern California Association of Governments, A Voluntary Advisory Forum of Cities and Counties," *op. cit.*, p. 1.
[26] *Ibid.*, p. 9.

mation systems; research; functional plans; comprehensive plan; citizen participation; comprehensive health planning; and regional criminal justice planning. The keystone of program activities is the identification and definition of regional planning issues, goals and objectives. The coordination of planning intends the "establishment of an appropriate framework for regional planning activities and studies encompassing related federal, state, and local agencies and citizen-based groups having regional planning interests."[27] Subsumed under these criteria is the fulfillment of research, analysis, and coordination of reporting in basic subject areas, such as population, economics, and land use; and the development and implementation of a regional information system program. SCAG is currently developing an information system which will consist of: (1) a regional planning library, (2) an internal information system for planning data, and (3) a program to coordinate regional information systems. Additionally, the Association is involved in the preparation of a regional comprehensive plan "which relates and integrates land use and functional plans in a comprehensive, long-range plan."[28] Finally, SCAG is in the process of coordinating the various development programs, and preparing functional plans including open space, water and waste management, and transportation, within the framework of the comprehensive regional plan.

Coordinative Model: Metropolitan Council of the Twin Cities Area. Pressured by an activist Citizens League and business groups for a regional functional authority for the Minneapolis-St. Paul area, and faced with the immediacy of a sewerage crises, the Minnesota legislature created the Council to coordinate the planning and development of the metropolitan area.

Behind formation of the council was a pressing but unglamorous need. As in most localities, the Twin Cities' post-war housing boom produced a sort of continuing crisis

[27] *Ibid.,* p. 10.
[28] *Ibid.*

of the sewers. By 1959, the area had some 300,000 individual wells and septic tanks. To avoid the harm to lakes and streams that individual municipal action could produce, the state legislature moved into the picture.[29]

The Council was created in an atmosphere of political sophistication which eschewed the more visionary, but practically deadly, notions of local unit consolidation into an all-purpose metropolitan government. The sensitivity to political realities dictated an avoidance of undertaking metropolitan consolidation, hence the state legislature, with the active backing of concerned citizens groups, opted for a Metropolitan Council with powers scrupulously delineated to functions of area-wide importance.

> But in those few fields where it would be given responsibility—sewerage and water supply, airport location, highway routes, preservation of open space, and the like—the Council would have real authority. It would have its own sources of revenue, so it would not have to depend on voluntary contributions from 150-odd municipalities. It would have responsibility for making overall plans "for the orderly physical, social and economic growth of the Twin Cities area." It could review all plans and projects of local government and special agencies, such as the Airport Commission . . . It also would be empowered to review local requests for federal aid.[30]

The Council has the functional authority to fashion a regional development plan, to intercede before the Minnesota Municipal Commission in annexation and incorporation determinations, to discharge research into pollution, the tax structure, waste disposal and open spaces, to operate a data center, and to review long-term plans of the local jurisdictions to insure conformity to area-wide formulations and coordinated activity. Its review authority is a compromise between unilateral direction and deference to home rule.

[29] "Where regional planners call the shots," *Business Week*, February 21, 1970, p. 72.

[30] John Fischer, "The Easy Chair: The Minnesota Experience: How To Make a Big City Fit to Live in," *Harpers Magazine*, April, 1969, p. 24.

When city plans, for example, affect the region, the council can hold them up to 60 days while it attempts to mediate and persuade. But it cannot halt them. On the other hand, where county boards and other agencies are concerned, the council can prevent action. Disputes that cannot be reconciled are sent to the legislature for resolution.[31]

The Council's planning responsibility encompasses a seven county area, which affects approximately 1.8 million people in Minneapolis, St. Paul, and 120 other communities. Its functional efficacy is a reflection of state legislative support, the formula for selecting council representation, financial independence, and authority to supervise the activities of subordinate agencies.

The Council is served by 15 part-time members appointed by the Governor for six year terms, and a full-time professional staff. Fourteen members represent state legislative districts in the Metropolitan Area, and the 15th member, the Chairman, is appointed at large. The fact that council members are not local elected officials encourages a regional perspective mitigating parochialism, city-suburban schism, and logrolling.

The state legislature has been responsive to the Council's needs and recommendations. The legislature granted the Council the authority to collect a regional tax and to issue bonds. In 1969, the Council collected $720,000 of its $1.6 million budget in taxes, with the balance ensuing from federal grants.[32] Additionally, following its first detailed report to the legislature in 1969, the Council was granted the added powers of involvement in regional highway planning, and the authority to set criteria and guidelines for land-use within three miles of a proposed new airport and to determine acceptable aircraft noise levels for each such land-use.

The legislature structured the Council as a general purpose coordinating agency for the multivarious special districts, and with real authority to make regional decisions. This

[31] "Where regional planners call the shots," *op. cit.* p. 73.
[32] *Ibid.*

has been effected by allowing the Council to establish its own operating subsidiaries to manage specific regional functions. Real, as opposed to advisory, control over the subsidiaries is realized through Council appointments of members of the subordinate bodies and approval of their plans and their finances. James L. Hetland, the Chairman of the Council, explained the program of intergovernmental coordination:

> [The Council] aims to serve as a kind of holding company, sketching out broad policy guidelines. It also will (he hopes) supervise a group of subordinate agencies which will carry out the detailed planning, construction, and day-to-day operaton of the regional facilities. Some of these already exist—for example, the quasi-independent Airport Commission and Transit Commission. Others will have to be created to handle such things as air pollution, garbage disposal, and—of all things—a zoo.[33]

Clearly, the Metropolitan Council is more than a model for functional coordination; it is exemplary of the reservoir of powers possessed by the state legislatures. The Minnesota example enlightens the potential of the states in the creation of appropriate institutions, in the financing of needed programs, and in the more effective conveyance of existing services. State legislatures have the latent ability to establish timely mechanisms to enable the rational management of the urban environment.

Authoritative Model: New York State Urban Development Corporation. New York State, influenced by the lobbying of Governor Nelson A. Rockefeller, chose, in 1968, to exercise its plenary powers and created an authority to deal with area-wide problems, the Urban Development Corporation (UDC). For the UDC to achieve its purpose of planning and developing the urban areas of the state, the legislature granted it extensive powers.

> The UDC can enter into joint financing agreements with local agencies or private groups. It has the power to float $1 billion in bonds. It can acquire land, both public

[33] Fischer, *op. cit.,* p. 28.

and private, through the exercise of eminent domain. It has the power to override obsolete zoning and building codes. It can provide the economic resources and expertise for the redevelopment of local communities and the construction of "new towns-in-town" and "new towns."

Above all, the Urban Development Corporation, unlike any other Government agency, has the major responsibility and the complete and continuing authority for the development of a project from land acquisition to final construction. The powers given to UDC enable it to deal with many of the complex problems—from start to finish —which thwart our housing and urban development programs.[34]

The Corporation is presided by nine directors, all appointed by the Governor, with the advice and consent of the New York State Senate. Four of the directors are chosen on the basis of positions already held in public agencies—Commissioner of Commerce, Superintendent of Banks, Superintendent of Insurance, and Director of the Office of Planning Coordination within the Executive Department—and five directors, one of whom is specifically designated chairman, are appointed at-large. The Governor establishes a business advisory council for urban development to provide guidance to the Corporation on matters of development policies and programs and to encourage the full participation of the private sector in Corporation projects. The Corporation, on its part, seeks the mobilization of public support and participation in projects affecting community development by forming community advisory committees. Furthermore, the Corporation is directed by law to maximize the utilization of local resources in affected project areas.

 The corporation shall take affirmative action in working with construction firms, contractors and subcontractors, labor unions and manufacturing and industrial firms, to to the end that residents of areas in which projects are to

---

[34] U.S., Congress, Senate, *Congressional Record, Proceedings and Debates of the 91st Congress, Second Session,* Vol. 116, No. 32 (Washington D.C.: March 4, 1970), p. S2988.

be located shall be afforded priority in the construction work on projects of the corporation, and in the business operations of tenants and occupants of industrial projects undertaken by the corporation.[35]

In addition to the pervasive UDC, with its ability to sell up to $1 billion of its own bonds, borrow money from the state Housing Finance Agency, and enter into joint ventures with public and non-profit developers, the development program also calls for the creation of two other, smaller corporations. Binding the three agencies is an interlocking board of directors.

One of the two smaller bodies is called the Corporation for Urban Development and Research of New York. It is financed through private gifts and grants, and through the sale of membership certificates and its own debentures and notes. This corporation is designed to carry out research seeking the development of new building materials and new techniques to optimize efficiency and minimize costs of construction. It is also responsible for the rehabilitation of small homes, or to extend loans for self-improvement, and can do some industrial rehabilitation and property acquisition for both industrial and housing needs. However, unlike the UDC, this agency does not have the power to condemn property or to override local zoning and building codes. Its sister corporation, the Urban Development Guarantee Fund of New York, obtains its capital similarly, and guarantees loans to small businessmen and homeowners for renewal and rehabilitation, if they are unable to obtain credit from conventional sources.

UDC's intent is to execute development programs . . .

. . . that will increase low and moderate income housing, help alleviate unemployment, revitalize industry, and expand community facilities—in cooperation with local communities and private enterprise.[36]

[35] "New York State Urban Development Act of 1968," Urban Development Corporation, Albany, N.Y., June, 1968, pp. 16–17.

[36] New York State Urban Development Corporation, *Fact Sheet* (mimeographed).

To accomplish these ends, Edward J. Logue, president and chief executive officer of the "most powerful agency ever assembled by any state government,"[37] has an amazing combination of powers at his disposal. Theoretically, UDC

> . . . is authorized by law to move into any community in the state, take whatever property it wants by condemnation, raze any structures on the site, and replace them wth homes, factories, schools, or office buildings, as it sees fit—all without paying any attention whatever to local zoning laws and building codes. It could put up a vast Negro housing project in the middle of Scarsdale, the richest white suburb in the state. It could build entirely new cities in the open countryside (and, in fact, already has three of them on its drawing boards). Furthermore, it has a lot of money; well over a billion dollars at its own command, and possibly another five billion of private investment to be spent under its direction.[38]

In actuality, however, the realities of political and market forces have been countervailing mechanisms against the potential of unrestrained abuse. Logue has displayed a political sagacity in his soothing away of the fears of John Lindsay and the state's other mayors of the agency's aggrandizement of home rule prerogatives. He promised the "political grandees" that UDC will never enter a community unless invited, to execute all projects in close consultation with local advisory committees, and to fully utilize existing resources for project implementation and operation. This intends the limiting of the Corporation's activities to planning, policy making, and stimulation of action by other sources.

To show the way he likes to operate, Logue points to a "memorandum of understanding" that UDC recently signed with suburban Westchester County outside New York City. Concluded after six months of talk, its two chief provisions are that UDC and the county will fund

[37] Ian Menzies, "Bay State Could Learn from New York," *The Boston Globe,* Sunday Globe, March 29, 1970.
[38] John Fischer, "The Easy Chair: Notes from the Underground," *Harper's Magazine,* February, 1970, pp. 12, 14.

a countywide development and that UDC will form a subsidiary corporation to carry it all out. Local officials will be named as the corporation's directors [appointed and dismissable by the UDC], providing the full benefit of local views . . .[39]

The goal of building sizeable tracts of low-income housing in hitherto unaffected preserves, has been handicapped by financial constraints as well as local hostility. UDC is not empowered to provide direct subsidies for low-cost housing construction. Instead, it relies on the sales of its bonds and, like private developers, must insure a sufficient return on its projects to retire the debt. Consequently, the proliferation of low-cost housing has been deterred by practical financial considerations, and a lack of funds for rent subsidies or urban renewal "write down" of land that reduces its cost at below market prices thus enticing private development.[40] At any rate,

> Logue says that [the agency] will use its wide range of compulsive powers (such as the power to override local zoning codes) "sparingly, so that our statute isn't repealed by the Legislature."[41]

As for subsidies, Logue considers this a federal, not a state responsibility, and would not hesitate to blame Washington should UDC fall short of its low-income housing goals.[42] Low-income housing is planned for 20 percent of new housing development, with 70 percent to be moderate-income, and 10 percent for the elderly.

UDC's projects posit dynamic undertakings, a good relationship with the state, and a direction toward the decentralization of jobs and people. The agency's preference for dispersed growth centers is a manifestation of its intent to

[39] "A Superagency for Urban Superproblems," *Business Week,* March 7, 1970, pp. 96, 98.

[40] *Ibid.,* p. 100.

[41] Richard Schickel, "New York's Mr. Urban Renewal," *New York Times Magazine,* March 1, 1970, p. 32.

[42] "A Superagency for Urban Superproblems," *op. cit.,* p. 100.

provide the state with new urban growth and development alternatives. Its projects involve the building of housing on vacant land and providing services and incentives to attract industry and population, and the renovation of existing settlements.

The UDC has approximately 45 studies and projects influencing the state's urbanization pattern,

> . . . including spectacular plans for three sizeable "new towns," or planned communities. One will be built on ramshackle Welfare Island, now a strip of drabness 2 miles long and 800 feet wide in New York City's East River; it may well transform the island into something like the Ile de la Cité, the historic heart of Paris in the River Seine, with shops, arcades, galleries, parks and housing for a brand new community of 20,000 people. The other two "new towns" will rise on a 2700-acre tract outside Syracuse and around the new state university campus in Buffalo.[43]

Newburgh's Lake Street project is an example of the UDC's program for a balanced revitalization of present communities. Prior to embarking on a new development, UDC requires the municipalities to contribute half of the cost for planning as a sign of "good faith"; Newburgh contributed $45,000 to this end. The proposal for Newburgh

> . . . called for 375 units of mixed-rental housing, to include the low-rent units and using federal interest subsidies, rent supplements and local tax abatement to produce moderate rents with state financing. Industry would occupy a specially-prepared part of the site. Construction would be by a private builder from the area. "UDC takes the costly early risks that discourage private developers," points out general manager Robert McCabe. "We're only builders in extreme. We do the planning, architectural design, feasibility studies, then say to private enterprise, 'Do what you can do best, build.'" The developer's mortgage would cover the several hundred thousand dollars in "front money" expended by UDC.

[43] *Ibid.,* p. 96.

At the [Newburgh project] ground-breaking—UDC's first—Rockefeller announced that two state highways would interconnect with the currently bypassing inter-state route, a link indispensable to Newburgh's revitaliza-tion. "When we look for help and support from the state we get it," says Logue.[44]

The New York model of a state-wide agency for urban management is a positive device for an ordered, rational al-location of people and resources. It is exemplary of a state's compulsory authority on behalf of a long-term planning con-sideration. The UDC experience is a reflection of one state's foresight in planning for community amenities as well as enhancing its attraction to market forces influential in urban development. Hence, the state, through its superagency, be-comes the instrument for environmental integration, offering well-planned and serviced locations for industry and its work force, thereby impelling a prescient governance over the destiny of its environment. It is, thus, reasonable to agree with Edward Logue that the first state with an integrated means for providing rational urban development "will be a quantum jump ahead of the rest."[45]

[44] Jeanne R. Lowe, "The States: Will They Act to Save Our Cities?" *Think*, published by IBM, March–April, 1970, p. 11.
[45] *Ibid.*, p. 12.

VII

The Making of
a Government

Modern systems analysis suggests that a socio-cultural system with high adaptive potential, or integration as we might call it, requires some optimum level of both stability and flexibility: a relative stability of the social-psychological foundations of interpersonal relations and of the cultural meanings and value hierarchies that hold group members together in the same universe of discourse and, at the same time, a flexibility of structural relations characterized by the lack of strong barriers to change, along with a certain propensity for reorganizing the current institutional structure should environmental challenges or emerging internal conditions suggest the need. A central feature of the complex, adaptive system is its capacity to persist or develop by changing its own structure, sometimes in fundamental ways.[1]

The linkage between the system and the environment are boundary-crossing transactions by way of inputs-outputs. These

[1] Walter Buckley, *Sociology and Modern Systems Theory*, (Englewood Cliffs, N.J.: Prentice-Hall, Inc., 1967), p. 206.

transactional processes of exchange are dependent upon reliable communication networks and information flows. Information is the regulator of the feedback loop and keys the political system to necessary behavior modifications and structural changes for coping with changes in the environment. Feedback enlightens the self-steering system about its proximity to objectives, thus enabling behavior modification, if required, for purposive goal-seeking. Management is the critical system component for the achievement of communication and control. Management is the information-processing function which converts data about system objectives, environment, components, and resources, into action outputs.

Management is the "steersman" of the political system. It generates plans for the system's execution, and insures their implementation. Management is the control center of the system's "cybernetic loop" with the environment. It institutes appropriate information systems in order to best evaluate the system's performance *vis a vis* its goals, and, through the feedback cycle, is able to correct goal-deviating execution. Hence, management is the fact-finding and action component indispensable to systemic transformation for persistence. However, systems management cannot provide its essential contributions to system persistence unless it is tied to the power foci of the political system. Fact-finding is often divorced from the action processes in the political system, thereby negating the potential attributes of efficacious control centers. Cybernetics feedback and action must be integrated; Kurt Lewin suggests that for fact-finding to be effective, it

> . . . has to be linked with the action organization itself: it has to be part of a feedback system which links a reconnaissance branch of the organization with the branches which do the action. The feedback has to be done so that a discrepancy between the desired and the actual direction leads "automatically" to a correction of actions or to a change of planning.[2]

Contemporary systems analysis intends the consideration of the overall system. The "meaning of a system" can be

[2] *Ibid.*, p. 173.

explicated in the context of its objectives, constraints, components, resources, and management. These are the crucial variables participating in system execution, and are causally linked to the morphogenic process of system adaptiveness to change. The interacting variables of the political system's "parts" offer an insight into its processes and capabilities for adaptiveness to the dynamic and unstable urban system.

Performance of the Political System
Through Its "Parts"

System Objectives

The actual performance of the political system has been less than paradigmatic of an adaptive, goal-seeking system. There has been appreciable concern articulated by political actors about the conditions of the urban system, and the past two decades have witnessed a proliferation of policy outputs and resources addressed to urban conditions. However, there has been a singular lack of coordination of outputs or purposive resource allocation. If anything, the multiplicity and fragmentation of outputs, albeit well-intentioned, have created a confusion within the political system without efficiently attending to the stresses in the urban system.

These outputs have usually been in the form of fiscal aid from the federal government to the states and local communities, to stimulate action on urban problems. The fiscal subvention has been engendered by a variety of legislation and programs. Unfortunately, each of these outputs had been enacted piecemeal—and oftentimes totally unrelated—to be administered by multifarious agencies, each requiring a bewildering assortment of compliance procedures.

The intensified activity at the national level of government has served to transform the character of the American federal system.

The total volume of federal aid to state and local governments more than tripled; between 1961 and 1966 alone, the Congress authorized federal assistance in 39 new fields of state and local activity. And this massive federal intervention in community affairs came in some of the most sacrosanct of all the tradtional preserves of state and local authority, such as education and, in 1968, local law enforcement.[3]

But, despite the rhetoric of national objectives, which peaked in recent times during the "New Frontier" and the "Great Society," the actual implementation of these goals has had to be executed by the officials in the country's myriad communities, "whom the federal government could influence—but not control."[4] The task of achieving goals promulgated by the central government through the operation of legally independent state and local governments, then, is a matter of coordination. Yet, it is not only a matter of coordination of the administration of national programs, but also a question of "bringing order to the maze of coordinating structures that federal agencies were independently propagating."[5]

The federal government has responded to the exercise of coordination at the local level by providing influences toward changing the structures and the distribution of influence in local government, in order to pursue nationally established goals. Parenthetically, the diseconomies of large-scale national bureaucracies and local demand for participation in public decisions have urged the movement toward the decentralization of federally defined and funded programs to subnational levels.[6] A meaningful development among the federal government's contributions to local structural innovation for purposes of coordination in behalf of national goals has been the prompting of a growth of regional institutions.

Along with the federal government's concern with structures appropriate for coordinated administrative management at the local level, has been the vexing problem of efficacious

[3] James L. Sundquist with the collaboration of David W. Davis, "Organizing U.S. Social and Economic Devolpment," *Public Administration Review,* No 6 (November/December, 1970), p. 625.

[4] *Ibid.*

[5] *Ibid.,* p. 626.

[6] Robert Warren, "Federal-Local Development Planning: Scale Effects in Representation and Policy Making," *Public Administration Review,* No. 6 (November/December, 1970), p. 584.

national level management of the overall system. The consideration of Executive-centered coordination and control evidences possibly the most noteworthy development in American public administration since World War II. The Nixon Administration's Reorganization Plan Number 2, creating the Domestic Council, and transforming the Bureau of the Budget into the Office of Management and Budget, with added responsibilities, is a significant attempt to provide integrated and systematic management. At the same time, the Administration has opted for a decentralized procedure of operational program coordination, by establishing the "federal region" concept for purposes of integrating administrative agencies' policies under the supervisory auspices of the newly-founded Office of Management and Budget.

It is premature to assess the possible effects of Reorganization Plan Number 2 and the federal region device, but meanwhile, the political system's cybernetic adaptiveness to its environment continues to be impeded by normative and practical constraints.

> A simple, cybernetic feedback model of explicit group goal-seeking does not fit most societies of the past and present because of a lack in those societies of informed, centralized direction and widespread, promotively interdependent goal behaviors of individuals and subgroups.[7]

System Constraints

The decentralized nature of the American political system, and a normative preference for the persistence of this phenomenon, posits dysfunctional attributes. The political system is characterized by a diffusion of decision centers which occasions the existence of several feedback loops, possibly contradictory, operating in the same system simultaneously. The multiplicity of unsynchronized and incompatible feedback cycles makes cohesive goal-seeking management, under existing conditions, unrealistic.

The unwieldiness of the diffused and expansive political

[7] Buckley, *op. cit.,* p. 206.

structure insures goal slippage during the course of implementation throughout the system. Goal-realization is impeded by the distance and quantity of linkages from the originating source. Practically, "goal decisions are translated by an administrative apparatus into concrete activities and rules of action to be applied by still another set of groups and individuals."[8] This would allow for deviations from original goal intentions, without explicit discernment of administrative failure or selective attention in output execution. The faulty cybernetic processes of multiple and differentiated linkages produces haphazard gathering and feeding back of information. Consequently, there exists an inevitable slack between action outputs and concrete manifestations of desired results.

The conditions involved in frustrating systemic goal-seeking through the cybernetic loop are also causal in blocking purposive structural changes. A rational delineation of state and local structures and functions, designed for mission-orientation, are subject to philosophic, legal, and political impediments throughout the system. The rigidity occurring in governmental units, fixed by normative and legal designations, encourages an irrelevance of present political structures to environmental problem-solving.

Finally, the political culture of the system has formalized parochialism in policy making and policy implementation. Fractionalization and compartmentalization of federal programs are the result of alliances between singular bureaucratic agencies and their congressional oversight committees. This relationship has led to an institutionalization of functional fiefdoms, each jealously guarded by an involved administrative agency and its congressional partners.[9] The phenomenon of functional fiefdoms has been particularly occlusive to the system's adaptive performance by its denial of an integrated treatment of programs.

---

[8] *Ibid.*, p. 175
[9] Harold Seidman, *Politics, Position, and Power, the Dynamics of Federal Organization,* New York: Oxford University Press, 1970.

System Components and Resources

In a systems analysis context, "missions" or "activities" are the components whose standard of performance truly narrates the performance of the overall system. The measure of a component's contribution to system performance is that if the standard of a component's performance increases, so should the standard of performance of the total system. In the political system, as constituted, there is no serviceable systems analysis of the whole system in terms of genuine mission-oriented components. This is particularly true at the state and local level where historical dictates have assigned governmental units with scant relationship to the true components of the system. Hence, because

> . . . the decision-making that governs different missions is not centralized, the real missions of the state, e.g., in terms of health, education, recreation, sanitation, and so on, cannot be carried out because there is no management of these missions.[10]

The components of the political system, albeit non-rationally defined, are made up of the myriad political, administrative, and judicial functional subsystems in the federal structure. And it is the specific actions taken by these subsystems in behalf of systemic goals which contribute to the measure of the total system's goal-seeking performance. Despite the essential characterization of the American political system as non-centralized, the supremacy of the national government has been assured by constitutional and environmental circumstances. Stresses in the environment leading to demands for effective public policy have been the centripetal influences compelling a political functional nationalization. The irresistible urge toward centralization of public policy has been occasioned by the national level's financial predominance and the states and local governments' oftentimes functional incapacity or indifference.

[10] C. West Churchman, *The Systems Approach* (New York: A Delta Book, Dell Publishing Co., Inc., 1968), p. 42.

The resources of the system are the general reservoir out of which the specific actions of the components can be formed. Hence, resources apply to finances, manpower, equipment, and information about the system and the environment. The 16th Amendment to the Constitution has given the national government a distinct financial advantage over the other levels, thereby instigating the focality of public policy. The national government's fiscal potency has also served to shape its preemption of professional talent and equipment. The states and localities, on their part, have either been legally restrained from expanding their resources, or have been remiss in developing new sources or in redefining their revenue-obtaining parameters.

Information about the system and the environment, a crucial variable for rational action by the system's components, has been randomly obtained because of the lack of coordination and control over the political system's many linkages. Despite the growth of centripetal tendencies in policy-making, the dearth of adequate systems management has dispelled the latent advantages of centralized mission direction. While several municipalities and other governmental institutions utilize some form of computerized information systems, there has been little attempt made to integrate information systems, or to prepare for a fully integrated information systems network by the ordering of standards for data congruity across department lines and between echelons of government. Ultimately, rational subsystem action through a feedback loop, for goal-seeking outputs adjustment, is dependent on coherent information systems.

Systems Management

The management of a system is the most important part of the system, for management engenders the plans fixing the component goals, allocating and utilizing the resources, and controlling the system's performance. Without appropriate planning and management the system operates in a random manner, much like a ship at sea without a steersman. The essence of systems management is administrative coordination, and logic dictates that the single point of leadership and coordination is in the national government, specifically in the Executive Office of the President.

Administrative coordination posits a process which integrates management and planning. Planning is a constituent phase of management for "it is not easy to separate the determination of objectives and the preparation of a course of action from consideration of the means of execution."[11] Yet, the function of government planning, particularly central government planning, has met with more hostility than any other government activity. To many people planning can only be defined as government direction of industrial production and distribution. But, in actuality, the

> . . . purpose of central planning in the federal government is comparable to the goal of comprehensive urban planning: a mutually consistent set of plans for many different government activities. The problem in central planning is not to produce plans; it is to bring all plans together at a central point where detailed proposals for action can be made to fit each other and at the same time to promote the realization of general national objectives. The job of central planning is to make sure that plans are prepared by operating agencies; that these plans are reviewed; and that the plans of any one agency do not come into conflict with the plans of another agency.[12]

The federal government's experience with centralized coordination and control was especially prolific during the New Deal and the subsequent war years. During World War II there occurred scant controversy about government planning. It was the national consensus, and basic national policy, that it was necessary to mobilize all national productive resources under the direction of the federal government in order to defeat the enemy. The War Production Board, established to this end, was granted control over raw materials, productive plants, prices, transportation, and labor.

[11] John D. Millett, *The Process and Organization of Government Planning* (New York: Columbia University Press, 1951), p. 87.
[12] *Ibid.,* p. 91

During this period of severe environmental stress, there were two additional coordinating arms at the Executive level, the National Resources Planning Board, and the Bureau of the Budget, created in 1939. However, in 1943, Congress signalled the demise of the NRPB by refusing any additional appropriations for the Board, and the House Committee on Appropriations stipulated a prohibition in the Independent Offices Appropriation Act, preventing the President from transferring any funds to the Board. The House's justification for its action was that the NRPB iterated the activities of other agencies. Hence, after August 31, 1943, the Bureau of the Budget was left as the sole coordinating arm of the Office of the President, for purpose of "insuring mutually harmonious plans."[13]

President Roosevelt, earlier in 1943, created the Office of War Mobilization by Executive Order. This agency was designed to

> . . . develop unified programs and to establish policies for the maximum use of the nation's resources in the war effort. It was directed to "unify" the activities of various agencies concerned with the production, procurement, distribution, and transportation of military and civilian supplies.[14]

After the obliteration of the NRPB, the President prescribed to the Office of War Mobilization the additional function of coping with war and postwar adjustment problems. In 1944 Congress added "and Reconversion" to the title of the Office of War Mobilization, and provided a statutory basis for the OWM's formulation of plans for the transition from war to peace.

> The directors of the OWMR were more than planners assisting the President; they were essentially coordinators of wartime and immediate postwar government activities, who gave much of their attention to the policy and planning phases of these activities.[15]

[13] *Ibid.*, p. 97.
[14] *Ibid.*, p. 152.
[15] *Ibid.*, pp. 156–157.

Its task of postwar reconversion completed, the agency ceased to function in December, 1946.

The Employment Act of 1946 created the Council of Economic Advisers. The Council's economic report to the President and the Bureau of the Budget's preparation of appropriation estimates were designed to provide the President with administrative efficiency controls. The Council of Economic Advisers, made up of three experts designated by the President, with the advice and consent of the Senate, were " 'to formulate and recommend national economic policy to promote employment, production, and purchasing power under free competitive enterprise.' "[16] The attention of the Council was to be primarily focused on the economic effects of government programs. The Bureau of the Budget was to be concerned primarily with the preparation of detailed appropriation estimates and with general administrative efficiency. But the Bureau went beyond its charter specifying it as the fiscal and management arm of the Presidency, and participated in the shaping of public policy because its Directors were convinced that resource management equated with influencing policy.[17]

On March 12, 1970, President Nixon released his Reorganization Plan No. 2 of 1970, calling for the creation of a Cabinet-level Domestic Council, and the transformation of the Bureau of the Budget into the Office of Management and Budget. The Plan was subsequently approved by Congress. The President's plan for organizational changes was devised to "make the Executive Branch a more vigorous and more effective instrument for creating and carrying out the programs that are needed today."[18] The Plan is the Nixon Administration's rationale for improving the management processes of the Executive Branch, by the careful coordination of programs, and an adequately informative information system.

---

[16] *Ibid.,* p. 160

[17] "Reorganization Plan No. 2: Remarks by Williams D. Carey," *Public Administration Review,* No. 6 (November/December, 1970), p. 631.

[18] The White House, "Reorganization Plan No. 2 of 1970," *Ibid.,* p. 611.

The Plan differentiates between the

> ". . . closely connected but basically separate func-
> tions" centered in the President's Office; "policy determin-
> ation and executive management. This involves (1) what
> Government should do, and (2) how it goes about doing
> it."[19]

With this perceived dichotomy spelled out, the reorganization
thus

> . . . creates a new entity to deal with each of these
> functions:
> —It establishes a Domestic Council, to coordinate policy
> formulation in the domestic area. This cabinet group would
> be provided with an institutional staff, and to a consider-
> able degree would be a domestic counterpart to the Na-
> tional Security Council.
> —It establishes an Office of Management and Budget,
> which would be the President's principal arm for the exer-
> cise of his managerial functions.
> The Domestic Council will be primarily concerned
> with *what* we do; the Office of Management and Budget
> will be primarily concerned with *how* we do it, and *how
> well* we do it.[20]

The Domestic Council will be chaired by the President,
and its membership will consist of the Vice President, and the
Secretaries of Housing and Urban Development, Health, Education, and Welfare, Treasury, Interior, Agriculture, Commerce, Labor, Transportation, and the Attorney General,
and the Director of the Office of Economic Opportunity.
Although the Council will operate with a staff under an
Executive Director, designated to be a Presidential assistant
in addition, the Plan contemplates having most of the substantive work done by *ad hoc* project committees—task forces,
planning groups, and advisory bodies—with the support of
the departmental staff. The intended functions of the Council
are as follows:

[19] *Ibid.,* p. 612
[20] *Ibid.*

—Assessing national needs, collecting information and developing forecasts, for the purpose of defining national goals and objectives.
—Identifying alternative ways of achieving these objectives, and recommending consistent, integrated sets of policy choices.
—Providing rapid response to Presidential needs for policy advice on pressing domestic issues.
—Coordinating the establishment of national priorities for the allocation of available resources.
—Maintaining a continuous review of the conduct of ongoing programs from a policy standpoint, and proposing reforms as needed.[21]

The Office of Management and Budget will still perform its predecessor's key function of preparing the annual federal budget and overseeing its execution, drawing on the transplanted career staff of the Bureau of the Budget, but this task will no longer be its dominant interest. The Plan emphasizes that the creation of the Office of Management and Budget is more than a mere change of name, but is basic to the broader management needs of the Office of the President. Hence, the new Office will apply greater stress on fiscal analysis, together with program evaluation and coordination, information and management systems, organizational improvement, and executive development, while maintaining its legislative reference service. To enable it to fulfill its increased responsibilities, the staff resources of the OMB will be augmented.

An additional emphasis of the OMB will be to respond to the need of developing and overseeing administrative coordinating mechanisms throughout the nation. The new federal region concept, inaugurated by the Nixon administration, provides for interagency coordination to be centralized in ten regional "capitals" and stimulated through Washington-based OMB "deskmen." Each federal region "capital" will house an interagency council coordinating administrative programs throughout its geographic jurisdiction which normally will encompass several designated states. The regional co-

21 *Ibid.,* p. 613.

ordination system will involve three departments—HUD, HEW, and Labor—and two agencies—the Office of Economic Opportunity and the Small Business Administration.

> Already a regional council, made up of the ranking field officers of each of the agencies, is in operation in every one of the regional headquarters. It selects its own chairman, and meets as often as necessary to thrash out mutual problems. . . .
> So far there is no resident representative of the President at regional headquarters, to knock heads together when necessary and make sure that White House policy is consistently carried out. But the Office of Management and Budget does have a "deskman" for each region, who pays frequent visits to the field. He is expected to mediate bureaucratic hassles on the spot, whenever possible, and to report back to Washington on the way each agency is doing its job.[22]

The administrative reorganization in the Executive Branch, coupled with the promulgation of the federal regions, posit major advances in the structural efficiency of the Presidency, and in intergovernmental coordination. It would be difficult for anyone concerned with Executive control and coordination to take issue with either the proposed functions of the Domestic Council, or with the new emphasis on management, program coordination, and fiscal and evaluative functions. However, there are logical inconsistencies and glaring omissions in Reorganization Plan No. 2, which require attention.

It is unfortunate that the Plan was conceived from a *Weltanschauung* of divided management functions, specifically: (1) what Government should do, and (2) how it goes about doing it. This criterion was applied in clearly defining the schism between the Domestic Council, which "will be primarily concerned with *what* we do," and the OMB, "with *how* we do it, and *how well* we do it." The reasoning of

[22] John Fischer, "The Easy Chair: Can the Nixon Administration Be Doing Something Right?" *Harper's Magazine*, November, 1970, p. 35.

this simplification is a casuistry; all evidence points to the un-reality of an organic separation of planning and policy shap-ing from resource management. Finally, for organizational *desideratum,* the non-inclusion of the Director of the Office of Management and Budget, the Chairman of the Council on Environmental Quality, and the Chairman of the Council of Economic Advisers, on the membership of the Domestic Council, is unconscionable.

The structural and functional innovations of Plan No. 2 and the federal regions signal a comprehension of the mag-nification of Executive managerial dimensions, and a need for strategic applications. The attraction of this development is not only in expectation of a departure from a prolonged bureaucratic inertia, but also in its germinal potential for fully-integrated communication and control throughout the federal system. The stresses in the urban system now require nothing less than the problem-solving facility of an adaptive, goal-seeking political system. This intends a political system which can regulate outputs from each succeeding subsystem in order to fashion an integrated flow.

Once before, under the compelling environmental con-ditions of World War II, American government was able to respond in a concerted goal-seeking attitude. This enabled us to defeat the enemy abroad. Now anew, compelling conditions in the environment require a dynamic, adaptive political system. We defeated the enemy then. Again we face a dangerous enemy, and he has been identified; in the immortal words of Pogo, "We have met the enemy, and he is us."

The task of integrating the political and urban systems for effective responsiveness to urban stresses and demands necessitates an adaptive political system. This intends action outputs within the context of integrated goal-seeking, goal-setting, communication, and control. Goals are then challenged under an uninterrupted cybernetic feedback loop. The ex-perience of the real political system evidences an unfulfillment of the paradigm. Utilizing the structural-functional reordering of Reorganization Plan No. 2 and the federal region device as the launching points for organizational evolution, the study is resolved with a systems model of an adaptive political system through the goal-directed execution of its governmental subsystems. The model is a heuristic scheme for the development of a self-steering, adaptive political system which provides conjunctive linkages with the urban system.

A Model of an Adaptive Political System
Total System Objectives, Management, and Constraints

The inefficiencies caused by the multiplicity of power centers and linkages in the political system, and the spotty performances of these diffused subsystems, tempts the expediency of a one-tier centralized, national government. This posits the eradication of the states as autonomous political units, and their replacement by Washington-appointed administrative components, strategically placed for organizational control efficacy.

The justification often placed for the abolition of the federal form of government is that the states have become a political *non-sequitur*. Although, it is correct that too many states have been remiss in the exercise of leadership and governmental perspicacity in numerous policy areas, this can also be said of the federal government, and no one has seriously advocated its dissolution. Furthermore, a careful examination of the political culture should immediately dispel any notions of a drastic structural metamorphosis.

The viability of government is based on the criterion of how well government serves the needs, and provides for the well-being of its constituents. If the political system fulfills these requisites it is assured of persistence; and, persistence is the *sine qua non* of the political system. But, in order for it to persist in the face of dynamic processes of environmental change, the political system must demonstrate a dynamic flexibility of its own, by an adaptiveness through structural and functional innovations, in search of new equilibria. The American political system is historically, legally, and culturally rooted in the framework of federalism. Persistence for the American political phenomenon is to adapt creatively to its environment, while retaining its essential federalism. It is within this context that the system persistence objectives operate.

The total system goal would be to provide control and communication for integrated inputs-outputs to serve desired contemplations of urban physical and activity patterns. This posits a strategic consideration of public policy influencing human activities, economic locational, activity, and investment alternatives, and social development. At the same time, the objective is to bifurcate the actual implementory components from the control focalities along a national-subnational, system-subsystem continuum. However, while the system-subsystem structures would offer functional differentiation, they would also be organically cohesive and integrated by mission linkages and cybernetic controls.

The total political system would retain its denationalized nature, but each subsystem would be organically linked to an ascending subnational control and communication center, up to a focality of strategic coordination located in the Executive Branch of the national government. This intends the "regionalization" of federalism, conceptualized as a five-tier federalist framework. The five tiers would be (1) the federal government; (2) the federal regions; (3) the states; (4) the metropolitan councils of government or regional planning institutions; and (5) the local jurisdictions.

Operationally, the system would operate in this manner: National agencies, at the Executive branch, would fulfill all of the intended activities described in President Nixon's Plan No. 2. The federal regions would retain their function of interagency coordination, but in addition, would be the subnational control and communication focalities for intergovernmental collaboration and coordination, as applied to inter-state and state-national government intercourse. In view of the increased responsibilities, the interagency council would be presided by a high-ranking resident executive responsible to a specified national management control agency. The national agency would provide the federal region councils with an operating staff, to include state "deskmen." The states would be the first-level "action" centers for the execution of urban strategies. The states, in effect, thus become the tactical arm of the federal regions. Their performance would be evaluated in terms of the quantity and quality of mission-outputs in response to total system goal objectives, and especially, in their stimulation of goal-seeking subsystem action agencies. The metropolitan councils of government and regional planning agencies are those action subsystems which would be responsible for the effectuation of authoritative outputs regarding urban area-wide considerations. The local communities would be expected to adhere to area-wide and state-wide goal formulations.

Goal formulation and attainment, and resources and components management are indissolubly linked, consequently, it is germane to depict the management process in the explication of system objectives. The realization of systemic self-steering is keyed to management as the steersman of the system. And management is the control and communication mechanism which strives for an integrated pattern of system-subsystem outputs to a desired terminal point. The focus of the management responsibility in the political system is in the Presidency. Thus, it is essential that the management process in the Office of the President be provided with the requisite tools for mission effectiveness.

The Domestic Council and the Office of Management and Budget are the structures designed for efficacious management. However, this model necessitates some fundamental changes in the functional parameters defined in Plan No. 2. Specifically, the dialectic of bifurcating planning and action would be eschewed. Instead, what would occur is that the Domestic Council would retain all of its prescribed functions, but the OMB would be designated as the collaborating agency responsible for the preparation of strategic plans for the Council. The guidelines for the planning of objectives would originate with the Council, and the OMB would design them accordingly. The OMB would be closely associated with the Council's operating staff for the planning of strategic national urban objectives, which subsequently would serve as policy options for the President and Congress. Of course, the Council, through its staff, would, in association with other involved agencies in the Office of the President, maintain a close liaison with Congress and provide all necessary assistance toward the fulfillment of requisite legislation and financing. Conversely, the legislative process, as well as the judicial, would serve as a check on imprudent behavior by these components and their agents. Finally, the Council membership would include the Director of the OMB, and the Chairmen of the Councils of Economic Advisers, and on Environmental Quality.

The federal region is the ideal geographic locale for the working-out of individualized patterns of relationships between the national government and particular states, and between states within the region. The formation of federal regions as federal government surrogates is an essential step toward the de-centralization of the national government. The regions embrace a large enough geographic area to provide a measure of comprehensive overview and control, while, at the same time, are sufficiently intimate to afford an appreciation for regional and local idiosyncracies.

Washington's representative at the federal region level would be a resident top-echelon executive of the OMB, assisted by a locally recruited staff. His duties would entail chairing interagency councils, and he would be charged with the authority and responsibility to speak for the national government in matters of intergovernmental relations and revenue-sharing. His office would be the recipient of block grants for subsequent subvention to the states or to lesser jurisdictions, according to strategic "missions" criteria. However, like the parent office in Washington, the federal region OMB would administer no substantive programs; it would be the communication and control center for the states in its jurisdiction, and the coordinating agency of intergovernmental programs in the region.

The states would be encouraged, by financial inducement, to establish agencies of state-wide program coordination, comprehensive planning, and urban development. The substantive mission-goals with which the states would be charged would include development of "new towns," transportation—specifically, rapid transit—environmental quality control, recreation, and open space and wildlife preservation. This would intend the creation of pertinent authoritative goal-action agencies; and their vigorous support at gubernatorial and legislative levels.

To encourage the importance and viability of metropolitan-region governmental and planning units, all revenue-sharing with the localities would be channeled through these agencies. They, in turn would allocate funds in accordance with missions related to area-wide comprehensive plans. The localities, however, would continue to receive grants-in-aid directly for territorially discrete missions. The local jurisdictions would be expected to provide inputs in the development of area-wide plans to be screened by a state comprehensive planning agency to insure compatibility with state-wide objectives.

Basic to management is communication. The hierarchy of management is connected by a communications network. It is the communication flow about the environment and about itself which enables systems management to effect control over its constituent parts, and to re-direct its processes according to goal feedback mismatch information. In effect, management is communications, and the quality of management is a product of the quality of its communications. Hence, the integration of the control centers at each level of the five-tiered federal system is dependent on a connecting chain of communications. Communication, in this sense, entails various forms: face-to-face contact, telephone, telegraph, letters, and so on. However, a cybernetic feedback loop requires a far more elaborate process of information flow. The enormous volume of data about the environment necessitates the utilization of the most up-to-date computer facilities. Therefore, a crucial element in the communication and control ability of the political system is its integration through a congruent management information system. This posits the utilization of extensive, computerized information systems.

The environmental constraints, as depicted in this study,

range from the mundane to the monumental. However, the ground-work for an incipient five-tier federal framework has already been set in Plan No. 2, and there has not been, as yet, serious opposition to its development. This is not to suggest that President Nixon has in mind the gradual evolution to the proffered model; it is only to put forth that adaptive processes stand a better chance of ultimate goal-fruition if cultivated incrementally. In the case of our model, procedural steps may be taken sequentially; for instance, the implementation of the information systems network, under auspices of federal government financing, would precede the expanded role of the OMB at the federal region, and so on. However, to foreclose the possibility of inchoate inertia, the five-tier federal framework should become operational within five years after the establishment of an integrated information systems network.

A legitimate criticism of the model is that it follows the form of federalism, but not its substance; that the OMB's role in the federal region is tantamount to that of the historic Roman proconsuls; and, that the federal region is prototypical of a European provincial government. And too, that the model anticipates the withering away of the federalist framework, as bureaucratic surrogates of the national government preempt the legitimacy of state governments. In fairness to this kind of an observation it must be admitted that the model poses a latent opportunity for an unrestrained evolutionary structural transformation of the total political system, its subtler intentions notwithstanding. In effect, the model poses a challenge to the components of the political system; a challenge which may be met by dynamic adaptive behavior along the system-subsystem continuum. The challenge of the state governments is especially compelling: whether we remain a federal republic may ultimately depend on their creative capacity for dynamism.

System-Subsystem Resources and Components Management

The most potent leverage possessed by the national government, on behalf of goal implementation, is its vast fiscal resources. It is through the proffering or withholding of grants that the federal government is able to induce its subsystems toward desired objectives. President Nixon, in his State of the Union Message of 1971, proposed that Congress legislate an unconditional revenue-sharing program with the states. While this concept poses benefits in terms of energizing state governments to unilateral action-programs, it is unfortunate from the standpoint of encouraging a disregard for strategically-defined considerations. By unconditionally relinquishing its major power resource, the federal government can expect to minimize its control effect on goal-seeking processes.

Instead, while committed to the concept of revenue-sharing, this model opts for a form of conditional disbursing. This would require the allocating of sizeable block-grants per federal region according to a per-capita and performance formula. The resident-director of the region's OMB would be charged with the authority and responsibility for allocating the fiscal resources to the separate states in his jurisdiction.

For a state to qualify for its share of the revenue it would need to meet several conditions, as defined by national strategic goals and OMB-defined state missions. If a state failed to meet these goals, then the OMB's federal-region "deskman" charged with "servicing" the affected state, would be assigned as OMB resident-coordinator within the state. He would establish an office in the state and deal directly with urban-region governments or planning regions located therein. Revenues earmarked for the state would come from the federal region, through the state's resident OMB coordinator, expressly for the urban-region institutions. The state government, however, although now ineligible for any portion of the block grant, could still qualify for its share of traditional grants-in-aid. But, of course, its chances for this revenue could possibly be lessened by the stigma of its ostracism from substantive programs by the federal region.

Generally, it is expected that most, if not all, states would fulfill their eligibility requirements and receive their block grant from the federal region. Some portion of the funds would be retained by the state government, for utilization in state-operated activities; the rest would be allocated, again in block-form, to the urban-region institutions. These, in turn, would retain a portion for their use, the rest to be parcelled out to the local jurisdictions. The eligibility for the state-meted out funds, in the case of the urban-regions, would be determined by an appropriate coordinating agency; the urban localities, last in line, would receive their disbursement according to the urban-region agency's prescription of mission requirements.

Fiscal resources are the means by which the linkage-centers effect control over the actions and performance of their charges. The development of an adequate feedback loop information system is the requisite for management communication. It is the coupling of these two aspects of management which enables goal-setting and goal-seeking to become realities. The exercise of management communication and control in contribution to integrated system outputs is basic to a cybernetic, adaptive system.

The establishment of management control-centers throughout the political system, by the strategic allocation of fiscal resources, would still fall short of system-subsystem integration, for until the control-centers are linked by an effective information network, they do not form a part of the cybernetic process. In the development of a fact retrieval computer-based information system, conducive to systemic management control integration, feasibility and hardware design should be important considerations. But, primarily, standards must be established immediately for data congruity throughout the information systems network. The design of the overall information system network should utilize the most current techniques, tempered by the "matrix" of anticipated information transactions within the system.

Because of the myriad system and subsystem components of the political system which would be interconnected in the information system network, and the huge volumes of data expected from these sources, the system could easily become very cumbersome and thereby, ineffectual. Therefore, it would behoove the political system to operate with as "streamlined" a network as possible, preferably within a real time, on-line retrieval context. The information system recommended to the state of California, in a study commissioned by Governor Brown in the early 1960's, is seductive by its simplicity. It would involve having components maintaining repositories of information files in various agencies with a central information component providing the basic information about where the data is stored.

> The remaining components consist of the linkages and terminals that connect the information requester to the central information system and thence to the files in which he is interested, as well as computer programmers located at each "data bank." [23]

The user of the system would have to specify the information requested by the use of a symbolic device, such as a code number, relayed to the central system, which would then direct him to where the information is located, or transmit his requisition to the appropriate agency.

Transformed to our model, this would involve the urban-region institutions as dynamic data acquiring, maintaining, and transmitting centers—or "data bases"—for the areas of their jurisdiction. The state governments would be the central information systems—keyed to information retrieval—linked to the larger information system at the federal regions. The federal regions would duplicate all the information retained by the linking states' central information systems. The national government would also be linked to the ten federal-region information centers. By the linking of all management control centers, and all those centers to other components, the system becomes amenable to a feedback loop relating to data about the urban system and about itself. However, the acquisition of non-quantifiable data, such as "happiness" data emanating from the members of the political system, undoubtedly, would still remain a matter of subjective assessment of environmental demand inputs.

[23] Churchman, *op. cit.*, p. 130.

The efficacy of the total system's goal-directed behavior is predicated upon the performance of its various components. A component's performance is measured by its sum contribution to mission accomplishment, through specific actions in behalf of system goals. This requires the designation of performance guidelines and evaluative criteria by the management control centers of the political system. In effect, this posits a management quality control requirement in a social-political system. In the model, system quality control is to be exercised at the subnational level of the federal regions. Subsystem quality control would be fashioned at the state level, and this activity would be performed down the line, potentially insofar as the subsystem components in the localities.

Component quality control is to be the device used by management control centers in the determination of block-grant subvention eligibility. In order to receive these funds each succeeding component will have to fulfill minimum performance criteria. Operationally, the federal regions would, first of all, expect a comprehensive plan drawn up by an appropriate state agency addressing itself to an ordered spatial and activity development in the state. The plan would also include substantive recommendations regarding environmental quality control, open space, "new towns," transportation, and other vital missions.

Next, the state government would show that it had created or elaborated fitting structures for the execution of the missions outlined in the plan. This is to say, the state government would have to demonstrate satisfactory progress toward the implementation of the comprehensive plan, by citing activities of state-wide agencies and other components. An example of an appropriate goal-seeking state-wide agency would be the New York State Urban Development Corporation; another representative component suitable for metropolitan area-wide coordination is the Metropolitan Council of the Twin Cities.

Finally, the state would have to evidence an energized expenditure of its own funds on plan-related missions, and a competence in enlarging its own resources. The latter manifestation could be demonstrated by an imaginative tax structure, to include one or more devices such as a state graduated-income tax, a state operated lottery, legitimized off-track betting, among several others. Once the state had obtained its share of the national financial resources it would then make its own allocations according to a discretionary quality control formula. The same procedure is to be repeated by succeeding block-grant distributors.

In effect, the five-tier federalism concept is based on the conceptualization of a supra-urban space defined in terms of delineated regions. The region is generally the spatial expression of linked physical and activity patterns. Hence, governmental control centers are defined in terms of appropriately sized regions for efficient servicing of these phenomena. The metropolitan region is the first unit of regional governmental endeavor; next, the state may not be a proper expression of interrelated activities and settlements, but it is scaled compatibly with a government-service region, and crucial to the scheme of systems management persistence because of its status of normative political legitimacy; and finally, the federal-region is the super-region designed for administrative expediency and the delivery of national government authority in a particularized, coherent fashion. The goal of their integration awaits an unravelling of the complexities of systems management through strategic goal-planning and an ensuing process of cybernetic communication and control.

National Strategic Goal-Planning

The urban region is a complex of linked centers of activity interacting through space. The basis for regional strategies is founded on the need for resolution of economic efficiencies, social satisfactions, space shortages, and urban design.[24] The maximization of economic efficiency intends a

[24] Derek Senior (ed.), *The Regional City, An Anglo-American Discussion of Metropolitan Planning* (Chicago: Aldine Publishing Co., 1966), pp. 39–40.

general development strategy which will equalize the distribution of resources, and provide for services at minimum cost; social satisfactions are obtained by ordering an environment with suitable compatibilities of the scale and spacing of communications, the location of facilities and workplaces, and the means of transportation; regional strategies must consider the shortage of space for an appropriate arrangement of activities and settlements, and anticipate the growth of population and activity; and, urban design must be ordered so as to provide for the best possible scheme for patterns of settlement to allow its inhabitants to optimize their human experience and potential for personal development. Hence, regional planning contemplates the integration of economic, social, and aesthetic factors and the devising of effective controls for their coordination.

The achievement of a balanced integration can only be fulfilled at the national level through appropriate policy and design in the elaboration of a strategy responsive to the holistic pattern of activity and interaction. Regions are the spatial expressions of these patterns indissolubly linked in super-space. Consequently, for a plan to be truly comprehensive, it must attach itself to a national spatial dimension which comprehends the regions as subsystems having internal balances and external flows. After all,

> . . . every regional definition is, of necessity, bound to a purpose derived from a national delineation of problems and goals, the definition is generally more mindful of what is socially valuable and politically significant than of scientific accuracy. Planning regions are best defined to be congruent in space with the socioeconomic functions to be carried out.[25]

The method by which to integrate the myriad activity flows and interdependencies is the formulation of a national

---

[25] John Friedmann and William Alonso, "National Policy and Regional Development," *Regional Development and Planning, A Reader,* Friedman and Alonso (eds.) (Cambridge, Mass.: The M.I.T. Press, 1964), p. 489.

urban policy. This is the process which affords a comprehensive respect for the wholeness of the spatial structure of development, in terms of both physical and activity patterns. A national urban policy focuses upon broader regional considerations, but planning on a national scale is founded on the prior attention given to regional needs. The basic allocation decisions are made with an awareness that problems and methods of development differ within each region despite the interdependence to a great extent of these allocations across all regional categories. Consequently, the very closest coordination of city and regional planning is essential for a definition of the urban problem, for "regional space is structured primarily through a hierarchy of urban places, and through the fields of interaction which relate them."[26]

From the aggregate inputs of coordinated city and regional plans, the national goals, standards, and priorities can be structured and the national interest rendered specific.

> [Decisions] must be made where, in what manner, and with what resources the national government is to support such urban activities as public housing, mass transit, sanitary works, and metropolitan highways.[27]

Finally, the national government can effect a strategic program for controls over the inter-spatial flows of resources and activities to coincide with regional tactics, in order to rationally manage the urban systems for the realization of a desired pattern of development.

The full utilization of the hierarchy of planning levels is indispensable to the coordination of activities. The hierarchy is essential to the feedback loop, initially as input devices articulating the urban condition to the national level, where these inputs are converted into policies of strategic controls which flow as outputs down through the succeeding echelons serving as conduits for their coordination and implementation. Thus, national strategic planning requires the mobilization of the many structures of administrative and

[26] *Ibid.,* pp. 65–66.
[27] *Ibid.*

political processes for the organization of supra-urban space to desired criteria.

The rationale for national controls over urban development is based on the Keynesian view of the economy as not a self-balancing mechanism, and applying it to the non-self-balancing urban realm. The urban realm is an organically interrelated system of people, economic activities, social institutions, and communications flows. Governmental intervention in the management of these activities is the injection of a countervailing force to frustrate the interplay of individual egoisms and their unwanted consequences. To do otherwise is to retain a governmental inertia in the face of mounting urban chaos, destruction of the physical environment, and the atrophy of the values and mores of civilization.

Bibliography

Books

Altschuler, Alan A. *The City Planning Process: A Political Analysis.* Ithaca, N.Y.: Cornell University Press, Cornell Paperbacks, 1969.

Annals of the American Academy of Political and Social Science. *Intergovernmental Relations in the United States.* Philadelphia: May, 1965.

Apter, David E. *The Politics of Modernization.* Chicago: The University of Chicago Press, 1969.

Babcock, Richard F. *The Zoning Game, Municipal Practices and Policies.* Madison: The University of Wisconsin Press, 1969

Bachrach, Peter. *The Theory of Democratic Elitism: A Critique.* Boston: Little, Brown & Co., 1967.

Baltzell, E. Digby. *The Protestant Establishment: Aristocracy and Caste in America.* New York: Random House, 1964.

Banfield, Edward C., and Wilson, James Q. *City Politics.* New York: Vintage Books, 1963.

Bellush, Jewel, and Hausknecht, Murray (eds.). *Urban Renewal: People, Politics, and Planning.* Garden City, N.Y.: Anchor Books, Doubleday & Co., Inc., 1967.

Blumenfeld, Hans. *The Modern Metropolis, Its Origins, Growth, Characteristics, and Planning.* Selected essays edited by Paul D.

Spreiregen. Cambridge: The Massachusetts Institute of Technology Press, 1967.

Bollens, John C., and Schmandt, Henry J. *The Metropolis: Its People, Politics, and Economic Life.* New York: Harper and Row, Publishers, 1965.

Buckley, Walter. *Sociology and Modern Systems Theory.* Englewood Cliffs, N.J.: Prentice-Hall, Inc., 1967.

Caiden, Gerald E. *Administrative Reform.* Chicago: Aldine Publishing Co., 1969.

Canty, Donald. *The New City.* New York: Published for Urban American Inc., by Frederick A. Praeger Publishers, 1969.

Chard, Jim, and York, Jon (eds.). *Urban America: Crisis and Opportunity.* Belmont, Calif.: Dickenson Publishing Co., Inc., 1969.

Chinitz, Benjamin (ed.). *City and Suburb, The Economics of Metropolitan Growth.* Englewood Cliffs, N.J.: Prentice-Hall, Inc., 1964.

Cities. (A Scientific American Book.) New York: Alfred A. Knopf, 1969.

Churchman, C. West. *The Systems Approach.* New York: A Delta Book, Dell Publishing Co., Inc., 1968.

Cleland, David I., and King, William R. *Systems, Organization Analysis, Management: A Book of Readings.* New York: McGraw-Hill Book Co., 1969.

Committee for Economic Development. *Reshaping Government in Metropolitan Areas.* New York: 1970.

———. *Guiding Metropolitan Growth.* New York: October, 1965.

Council of State Governments. *The States and the Metropolitan Problem, a Report to the Governors' Conference.* Chicago: 1956.

Crouch, Winston W., and Dinerman, Beatrice. *Southern California Metropolis, A Study in Development of Government for a Metropolitan Area.* Berkeley, Calif.: University of California Press, 1963.

Dahl, Robert A. *Who Governs? Democracy and Power in an American City.* New York: Yale University Press, 1961.

Deutsch, Karl W. *The Nerves of Government, Models of Political Communication and Control.* New York: The Free Press: 1966.

Easton, David. *A Systems Analysis of Political Life.* New York: John Wiley and Sons, Inc., 1967.

———, (ed.). *Varieties of Political Theory.* Englewood Cliffs, N.J.: Prentice-Hall, Inc., 1966.

Ehrlich, Dr. Paul R. *The Population Bomb.* New York: Ballantine Books, 1969.

Elazar, Daniel J., and others (eds). *Cooperation and Conflict, Readings in American Federalism.* Itasca, Ill.: F. E. Peacock Publishers, Inc., 1969.

Eldredge, H. Wentworth (ed.). *Taming Megalopolis,* Vol. I: *What Is and What Could Be.* Vol. II: *How to Manage an Urbanized*

World. Garden City, N Y.: Anchor Books, Doubleday & Co., Inc., 1967.

Ewald, William R., Jr. (ed.). *Environment For Man, The Next Fifty Years*. Bloomington: Indiana University Press, 1967.

———. *Environment and Policy, The Next Fifty Years*. Bloomington: Indiana University Press, 1968.

Fiser, Webb S. *Mastery of the Metropolis*. Englewood Cliffs, N.J.: Prentice-Hall, Inc., A Spectrum Book, 1962.

Forrester, Jay W. *Urban Dynamics*. Cambridge: The Massachusetts Institute of Technology Press, 1969.

Friedmann, John, and Alonso, William (eds.). *Regional Development and Planning, A Reader*. Cambridge: The Massachusetts Institute of Technology Press, 1964.

Friend, J. K., and Jessop, W. N. *Local Government and Strategic Choice, An Operational Research Approach to the Processes of Public Planning*. London: Tavistock Publications, 1969.

Goldman, Marshall I. (ed.). *Controlling Pollution: The Economics of a Cleaner America*. Englewood Cliffs, N.J.: Prentice-Hall, Inc., 1967.

Goldschmidt, Walter. *Comparative Functionalism: An Essay in Anthropological Theory*. Berkeley and Los Angeles: University of California Press, 1966.

Goodman, William I., and Freund, Eric C. (eds.). *Principles and Practice of Urban Planning*. Washington, D.C.: International City Managers Association, Municipal Management Series, 1968.

Goodman, Percival and Paul. *Communitas, Means of Livelihood and Ways of Life*. New York: Vintage Books, 1960.

Grodzins, Morton. *Goals for Americans*. Englewood Cliffs, N.J.: Prentice-Hall, Inc., 1968.

Gulick, Luther Halsey. *The Metropolitan Problem and American Ideas*. (Five Lectures delivered on the William W. Cook Foundation at the University of Michigan, March 6–10, 1961.) New York: Alfred A. Knopf, 1966.

Hare, Van Court, Jr. *Systems Analysis: A Diagnostic Approach*. New York: Harcourt, Brace and World, Inc., 1967

Hayek, Friedrich A. *The Road to Serfdom*. Chicago: The University of Chicago Press, Phoenix Books, 1967.

Heady, Ferrel. *Public Administration: A Comparative Perspective*, Foundations of Public Administration Series. Englewood Cliffs, N.J.: Prentice-Hall, Inc., 1966.

Heer, David M. *Society and Population*. Englewood Cliffs, N.J.: Prentice-Hall, Inc., 1968.

Herber, Lewis. *Crisis in Our Cities*. Englewood Cliffs, N.J.: Prentice-Hall, Inc., 1965.

Isard, Walter, in association with Smith, Tony E. and Isard, Peter; Tung, Tze Hsiung; Dacey, Michael. *General Theory, Social, Political, Economic, and Regional with particular Reference to*

Decision-Making Analysis. Cambridge: The Massachusetts Institute of Technology Press, 1969.

Johnson, Richard A., Kast, Fremont E., and Rosenzweig, James E. *The Theory and Management of Systems.* New York: McGraw-Hill, 1963.

Kaplan, Harold. *Urban Political Systems: A Functional Analysis of Metro Toronto.* New York: Columbia University Press, 1967.

Kent, T. J., Jr. *The Urban General Plan.* San Francisco: Chandler Publishing Co., 1964.

Kerlinger, Fred N. *Foundations of Behavioral Research.* New York: Holt, Rinehart & Winston, Inc., 1965.

Kornhauser, William. *The Politics of Mass Society.* The Free Press of Glencoe, Illinois, 1959.

Lasswell, Harold. *Politics: Who Gets What, When, How.* Cleveland: The World Publishing Co., Meridian Books, 1968.

MacIver, R. M. *The Web of Government.* Revised edition. New York: The Free Press, 1965.

Martindale, Don (ed.). *Functionalism in the Social Sciences: The Strength and Limits of Functionalism in Anthropology, Economics, Political Science, and Sociology.* (Monograph 5.) Philadelphia: The American Academy of Political and Social Science, February, 1965.

Marx, Herbert L. (ed.). *Community Planning.* (The Reference Shelf, Vol. 28, No. 4.) New York: H. W. Wilson Co., 1956.

Meehan, Eugene J. *Contemporary Political Thought: A Critical Study.* Homewood, Ill.: The Dorsey Press, 1967.

Meyerson, Martin, and Banfield, Edward C. *Politics, Planning, and the Public Interest: The Case of Public Housing in Chicago.* New York: Crowell-Collier Publishing Co., The Free Press of Glencoe, 1964.

Millett, John D. *The Process and Organization of Government Planning.* New York: Columbia University Press, 1951.

Mitchell, William C. *The American Polity: A Social and Cultural Interpretation.* New York: The Free Press, 1970.

Monsma, Stephen V. *American Politics: A Systems Approach.* New York: Holt, Rinehart, and Winston, Inc., 1969.

Morton, Robert K. *Social Theory and Social Research.* Glencoe, Ill.: Free Press, 1957.

Parsons, Talcott. *The Structure of Social Action.* New York: McGraw-Hill, Inc., 1937.

Perloff, Harvey S. *Education for Planning: City, State, and Regional.* Baltimore: The Johns Hopkins Press, for Resources for the Future, Inc., 1958.

——— (ed.). *The Quality of the Urban Environment: Essays on "New Resources" in an Urban Age.* Baltimore: The Johns Hopkins Press, for Resources for the Future, Inc., 1969.

Polsby, Nelson W. *Community Power and Political Theory.* New Haven, Conn.: Yale University Press, 1967.

Presthus, Robert. *Men at the Top: A Study in Community Power.* With a chapter by L. Vaughn Blankenship. New York: Oxford University Press, 1964.

Rabinovitz, Francine F. *City Politics and Planning.* New York: Atherton Press, 1969.

Reagan, Michael D. (ed.) *The Administration of Public Policy.* Glenview, Ill.: Scott, Foresman and Co., 1969.

Rodwin, Lloyd. *Nations and Cities: A Comparison of Strategies for Urban Growth.* Boston: Houghton-Mifflin Co., 1970.

Rose, Arnold M. *The Power Structure: Political Process in American Society.* New York: Oxford University Press, 1967.

Rossiter, Clinton. *1787: The Grand Convention.* New York: The MacMillan Co., 1966.

Sanford, Terry. *Storm Over the States.* New York: McGraw-Hill, 1967.

Schmandt, Henry J., and Bloomberg, Warner, Jr. (eds.). *The Quality of Urban Life.* Vol. III: *Urban Affairs Annual Reviews.* Beverly Hills, Calif.: Sage Publications, Inc., 1969.

Schorr, Alvin L. *Explorations in Social Policy.* New York: Basic Books, Inc., 1968.

Science, Engineering and the City. (A symposium sponsored jointly by the National Academy of Sciences and the National Academy of Engineering.) Washington, D.C.: National Academy of Sciences Publications 1498, 1967.

Scott, Stanley, and Bollens, John C. *Governing a Metropolitan Region: San Francisco Bay Area.* Institute of Governmental Studies, University of California, Berkeley, 1968.

Scott, Stanley (ed.), *The San Francisco Bay Area, Its Problems and Future.* Vol. II. Institute of Governmental Studies, University of California, Berkeley, 1966.

Seidman, Harold. *Politics, Position, and Power: The Dynamics of Federal Organization.* New York: Oxford University Press, 1970.

Senior, Derek (ed.). *The Regional City: An Anglo-American Discussion of Metropolitan Planning.* Chicago: Aldine Publishing Co., 1966.

Sharkansky, Ira (ed.). *Policy Analysis in Political Science.* Chicago: Markham Publishing Co., 1970.

Shepard, Paul, and McKinley, Daniel (eds.). *The Subversive Science: Essays Toward an Ecology of Man.* Boston: Houghton Mifflin Co., 1969.

Shils, Edward, *Political Development in the New States.* The Hague: Mouton & Co., 1962.

Smith, Harold D. *The Management of Your Government.* New York: McGraw-Hill Books Co., 1945.

Sweeney, Stephen B., and Charlesworth, James C. *Governing Urban Society: New Scientific Approaches.* (Monograph 7). Philadelphia: The American Academy of Political and Social Science, May, 1967.

Udall, Stewart L. *The Quiet Crisis.* New York: Holt, Rinehart & Winston, 1963.

Webber, Melvin M., and others. *Exploration into Urban Structure.* Philadelphia: University of Pennsylvania Press, 1964.

Wood, Robert C. *Metropolis Against Itself.* New York: Committee for Economic Development, 1959.

Zimmerman, Joseph F. (ed.). *Government of the Metropolis: Selected Readings.* New York: Holt, Rinehart & Winston, Inc., 1968.

———. *1968 Metropolitan Area Annual.* Albany, N.Y.: Graduate School of Public Affairs, State University of New York at Albany, 1968.

Articles and Periodicals

"A Superagency for Urban Superproblems," *Business Week,* March 7, 1970.

Adelson, Marvin. "The Systems Approach—A Perspective," *SDC Magazine,* October, 1966.

Banfield, Edward C. "The Politics of Metropolitan Area Organization," *Midwest Journal of Political Science,* May, 1957.

Barrett, Steve. "The Cities: Meeting the Crisis," *SDC Magazine,* XXII, No. 10 December, 1969.

"City-County Consolidation: Trend for the 1970's?" *Nation's Cities,* November, 1969.

"County Provides Municipal Services on Contract Basis," *Better Roads,* April, 1970.

Ekistics. Reviews on the problems and science of human settlements, XX No. 116 July, 1965.

Fischer, John. "The Easy Chair: Can the Nixon Administration Be Doing Something Right?" *Harper's Magazine,* November, 1970.

Fischer, John. "The Easy Chair: Notes from the Underground," *Harper's Magazine,* February, 1970.

Fischer, John. "The Easy Chair: The Minnesota Experience: How To Make a Big City Fit to Live In, *Harper's Magazine,* April, 1969.

Friedmann, John. "The Future of Comprehensive Urban Planning: A Critique," *Public Administration Review,* No. 3, May/June, 1971.

Hertz, David B. "Computers and the World Comunications Crisis," *The American Scholar,* Spring, 1966.

Jordan, Gerald. "Three Models of Political and Social Thought," *Administrative Law Review,* XXII June, 1970.

Lessing, Lawrence. "Systems Engineering Invades the City," *Fortune,* LXXVII, No. 1 (January, 1968).

Lewis, Anthony. "Technology on Environment: A Choice Has to Be Made," *Riverside Daily Enterprise*, Nov. 17, 1969.

Lowe, Jeanne R. "The States: Will They Act to Save Our Cities?" *Think* (published by IBM), March–April, 1970.

Lowi, Theodore. "Toward Functionalism in Political Science: The Case of Innovation in Party Systems," *The American Political Science Review*, LVII September, 1963.

McLuhan, Herbert Marshall. "Address at Vision 65," *The American Scholar*, Spring, 1966.

Menzies, Ian. "Bay State Could Learn from New York," *The Boston Globe*, Sunday Globe, March 29, 1970.

Middleton, John T. "Man and His Habitat: Problems of Pollution," *Bulletin of the Atomic Scientists*, March, 1965.

——, and Diana C. "Motor Vehicle Pollution Control," *Traffic Quarterly*, April, 1961.

——. "Air Pollution and California's State Control Program. (Abstract published by the University of California, Riverside, State-wide Air Pollution Research Center), 1962.

"Reorganization Plan No. 2: Remarks by William D. Carey," *Public Administration Review*, No. 6 November/December, 1970.

Rosenblith, Walter A. "On Cybernetics and the Human Brain," *The American Scholar*, Spring, 1966.

Ruff, Larry E. "Price Pollution Out of Existence," Topical Comment: Practical Attack, *Los Angeles Times*, Dec. 7, 1969.

Schickel. "New York's Mr. Urban Renewal," *New York Times Magazine*, March 1, 1970.

Sundquist, James L., with the collaboration of David W. Davis. "Organizing U.S. Social and Economic Development," *Public Administration Review*, No. 6 November/December, 1970.

The White House, "Reorganization Plan No. 2 of 1970," *Public Administration Review*, No. 6 November/December, 1970.

von Eckardt, Wolf. "The Perils of Concentration," *Saturday Review*, May 2, 1970.

Warren, Robert. "Federal-Local Development Planning: Scale Effects in Representation and Policy Making," *Public Administration Review*, No. 6 November/December, 1970.

"Where Regional Planners Call the Shots," *Business Week*, February 21, 1970.

Zimmerman, Joseph F. "Metropolitan Reform in the U.S.: An Overview," *Public Administration Review*, September/October, 1970.

Reports

American Institute of Planners. California Chapter Regional Planning Committee, "The Scope and Methodology of Regional Planning, A Position Paper," January 3, 1969.

"A Municipal Information and Decision System, Vol. II, Vertical Subsystem," Municipal Systems Research. Los Angeles: University of Southern California, School of Public Administration, 1968.

Graduate School of Public Affairs, State University of New York at Albany. "1968 Survey of Metropolitan Planning," New York, 1968.

Management Information Service. "Introduction to Systems Analysis." Conducted by the International City Managers' Association, Report No. 198, Washington, D.C., November, 1968.

Middleton, John T. *Science and Environmental Control, Smog-Free Air and Its Price*. Proceedings of Symposium on "California and Challenge of Growth," University of California, San Diego, June, 1963.

National Service to Regional Councils. "Regional Alternatives," Special Report #2, Washington, D.C., May, 1968.

——. "Organizing a Regional Council," Special Report #3, Washington, D.C., May, 1968.

——. "Regional Council Bylaws," Special Report #4, Washington, D.C., May, 1968.

——. "Regional Program Primer," Special Report #5, Washington, D.C., July, 1968.

National Service to Regional Councils. "Program Implementation," Special Report #6, Washington, D.C., July, 1968.

——. "Key Federal Programs," Special Report #7, Washington, D.C., July, 1968.

——. "Regional Councils and the States," Special Report #8, Washington, D.C., July, 1968.

New York State Urban Development Corporation, *Fact Sheet* (Mimeographed).

Quade, E. S. "The Systems Approach and Public Policy," P-4053, The RAND Corporation, Santa Monica, Calif., March, 1969.

Southern California Association of Governments. *A Voluntary Advisory Forum of Cities and Counties,* SCAG, February, 1969.

Other Sources

California Council on Intergovernmental Relations. Letter to: City Councils and Boards of Supervisors in the State of California, "Policy Statement on Regional Organization," Sacramento, California, December 1, 1969, and May 9, 1969 (mimeographed).

——. "Regional Organization, Background Paper for Council on Intergovernmental Relations," Sacramento, California, May 8, 1969 (mimeographed).

California State Clearinghouse, Office of Intergovernmental Management. Memorandum from Lieutenant Governor Ed Reinecke, Sacramento, California, June 18, 1970 (mimeographed).

——. "Grant Review Procedures and Forms," Sacramento, California, April 15, 1970 (mimeographed).

Executive Office of the President, Bureau of the Budget. Circular No. A-95, Washington, D.C., July 24, 1969 (mimeographed).

————. Circular No. A-82, Washington, D.C., April 11, 1967 (mimeographed).

"New York State Urban Development Act of 1968," Urban Development Corporation, Albany, N.Y., June, 1968.

National Association of Regional Councils. Washington, D.C.: Letter, March 14, 1972.

U.S. Advisory Commission on Intergovernmental Relations, Washington, D.C.: Letter, March 8, 1972.

Unpublished Material

Anderson, Anthony H. "The Movement Towards Regional Government," Unpublished Master's Thesis, Department of Government, Claremont Graduate School, Claremont, California, April, 1970.

Public Documents

Hanson, Royce, for the Advisory Commission on Intergovernmental Relations. *Metropolitan Councils of Government: An Information Report.* August, 1966.

U.S. Advisory Commission on Intergovernmental Relations. *Factors Affecting Voter Reactions to Governmental Reorganization in Metropolitan Areas.* Summary of Report M-15. September, 1965.

————. *Urban and Rural America: Policies for Future Growth,* A-32. April, 1968.

————. *Urban America and the Federal System, Commission Findings and Proposals,* M-47. October, 1969.

U.S. Census Bureau. 18th Census, 1960, U.S. Census of Population, *Standard Metropolitan Statistical Areas.*

U.S. Congress. *Building the American City, Report of the National Commission on Urban Problems to the Congress and to the President of the United States.* 91st Cong., 1st Sess., House, Document No. 91-34 December 12, 1968.

U.S. Department of Commerce. *County and City Data Book, 1967.*

U.S. Department of Health, Education, and Welfare, Public Health Service. *Air Pollution . . . A National Problem.* Prepared for the National Conference on Air Pollution, December 10-12, 1962.

————. Consumer Protection and Environmental Health Service, National Air Pollution Control Administration, *Report for Consultation on the Metropolitan Los Angeles Air Quality Control Region.* November, 1968.

U.S. Government. Report of the Environmental Pollution Panel, The President's Science Advisory Committee, *Restoring the Quality of Our Environment.* The White House, November, 1965.

U.S. Government. The President's Council on Recreation and Natural Beauty. *From Sea to Shining Sea: A Report on the American Environment—Our Natural Heritage,* 1968.

U.S. House of Representatives. A Study Submitted to the Intergovernmental Relations Subcommittee of the Committee on Government Operations by the Advisory Committee on Intergovernmental Relations, *Metropolitan America: Challenge to Federalism*. 89th Cong., 2d Sess., October, 1966.

U.S. Senate, Congressional Record. *Proceedings and Debates of the 91st Congress, Second Session*. Vol. 116, No. 32, March 4, 1970.

U.S. Senate, Subcommittee on Intergovernmental Relations of the Committee on Government Operations, in Cooperation with the Joint Center for Urban Studies of the Massachusetts Institute of Technology and Harvard University. *The Effectiveness of Metropolitan Planning*. 88th Cong., 2d Sess., June 30, 1964.

Index

F1